THE SECOND WORLD WAR IN 100 FACTS

CLIVE PEARSON

*This book is dedicated to my patient and
long-suffering wife, Anya*

First published 2017

Amberley Publishing
The Hill, Stroud
Gloucestershire, GL5 4EP

www.amberley-books.com

British Library Cataloguing in Publication Data.
A catalogue record for this book is available from the British Library.

ISBN 978 1 4456 5353 2 (paperback)
ISBN 978 1 4456 5354 9 (ebook)

Typeset in 11pt on 13pt Sabon.
Origination by Amberley Publishing.
Printed in the UK.

CONTENTS

Introduction

If the First World War was not truly global in its embrace then the Second World War came much closer to achieving this. Japanese ambitions resulted in vast swathes of the Far East and the Pacific becoming embroiled and this meant that this war was not just about a struggle centred on Europe as in the previous conflict. With particular regard to the European theatre, however, the Second World War is seen by many as a continuation of the first with a 'Twenty Years' Truce' in between. Interestingly, there are certainly many similarities; for example, both wars started in Eastern Europe, both began with an alliance of Britain and France bent on denying Germany her imperial ambitions, and both wars were finally won by a grand alliance of Britain, France, Russia and the USA.

Of course, the two wars did have clear differences. To begin with it was France not Russia that suffered defeat and occupation. Above all the Second World War was a struggle between ideologies. On the one side you had the extreme right-wing forces of Nazism, Fascism and Japanese militarism and on the other Communism and liberal democracy (the latter two were rather unfamiliar bedfellows). Perhaps more than any other previous wars the belligerents were engaged in a race for technological innovation. The war resulted in the development of rocketry, the jet engine and the atomic bomb. We must not forget too that the Second World War was a racial war; both Germany and Japan were determined to set themselves up as racial superiors over those they conquered. In the case of Nazi Germany this extended into genocidal policies resulting in the deaths of 6 million Jews and 27 million Russians. Overall, the war was much bloodier than previous conflicts, with an estimated 50 million people losing their lives.

You may well ask if it was inevitable that the Allies would win. On paper this would seem to be the case. The Axis powers and Japan were taking on the might of the most powerful country in the world (the United States), the country with the largest empire in the world (Great Britain) and the largest country in the world (the Soviet Union). Indeed, the production figures of America alone dwarfed that of the enemy powers. However, nothing is certain in war. Allied victories sometimes came about by the narrowest of margins. Apart from the massive resources at their disposal, the Allies also helped their cause by operating much more closely together and by having better command structures. (The German armed forces were dependent on the whims of one rather unhinged dictator for their orders.) More importantly, they effectively harnessed their peoples into a moral crusade to destroy the forces of terror and oppression.

There have been countless books published on the Second World War. As in all the other books in the 100 Facts series, this book is intended as a gentle introduction to the topic. You don't have to devour it all in one sitting. You can, if you prefer, take it in easy stages, perhaps accompanied by a light beverage. Whichever is your preference I hope you enjoy reading it.

1. Appeasement Was Not the Easy-Peasy Option

During the 1930s Britain and France had a choice in their foreign policy. Either they could confront the dictators (in particular Germany's Adolf Hitler) or they could seek to avoid a war by trying to offer the dictators what they wanted within acceptable limits. This latter option was dubbed 'appeasement', which was explained as giving in to the 'just grievances' of the dictators and thereby creating a lasting peace.

This policy is mostly associated with the British Prime Minister Neville Chamberlain. However, he was not alone. He carried most of the establishment with him and only a few voices, such as that of Winston Churchill, denounced it. However, it is perhaps rather unkind to describe it as the soft option. British and French leaders were constrained very much by public opinion in their respective countries. The carnage and terrible losses of the First World War, which had ended in 1918, were still fresh in people's minds. The French had said '*jamais plus*' (never again) to a European war and this was also an opinion widely held in Britain. In addition, Britain in particular had scaled back her army and air force as part of the peace dividend and felt unready for a war. Above all, Chamberlain naively believed that Hitler and his ally, the Italian dictator Benito Mussolini, were people that could be trusted once their demands had been met. Unfortunately, it didn't quite work out like that. Once one piece of territory had been gobbled up and digested, the dictators came back greedily for more. This scenario is all too well illustrated by Hitler's adept exploitation of this appeasement policy. When in 1936 German forces boldly reoccupied the Rhineland, this was deemed justifiable by Britain as the Versailles Treaty of 1919 was felt to have been overly harsh on Germany. However, Hitler had been prepared to make a rapid withdrawal had he been confronted. When Germany annexed Austria in March 1938 it was justified because Austrians were fellow Germans who wanted to join the Reich. Hitler used the same excuse in September when he demanded Sudeten Germans should be allowed to join Germany. Shamefully, at Munich Britain and France agreed and left Czechoslovakia stripped of her border defences. Afterwards the dictator solemnly pronounced that he had no more territorial ambitions in Europe. Upon his arrival back in Britain Chamberlain unveiled a piece of paper with Hitler's guarantee and declared there was 'peace in our time!' Alas for Chamberlain and the people of Europe, six months later the Führer broke his promise by unceremoniously marching his armies into Prague and breaking up the Czechoslovak state. This time, though, there could be no more justification as few Germans lived there.

At this juncture even Chamberlain realised that Hitler was a ruthless aggressor with limitless ambitions. Hitler had clearly broken his trust. It marked a turning point in the policy of appeasement. When, in September 1939, Hitler invaded Poland the Allies, Britain and France, perhaps rather belatedly, declared war on Germany.

2. Britain Didn't Just Go to War to Defend Poland

The reader may have previously been bemused by the thought that Britain declared war on Germany to defend a country that it had little hope of liberating; indeed Poland stayed firmly under Nazi control for most of the war before swiftly passing under the Soviet boot. The real reason, then, must surely lie elsewhere.

Back in 1939 Britain still had her world empire and considered herself to be a 'great power'. Germany was threatening to dominate the Continent and thereby threaten that very status. The invasion of Poland can be seen, then, as the occasion for Britain going to war in order to defend her position. The cause had been building for some years.

By March 1939 it was clear that the appeasement policy had failed and that the Allies, Britain and France, had to prepare for war. However, British Prime Minister Neville Chamberlain had not been negligent regarding Britain's armed forces. Britain's air and sea forces had been in the process of renovation over the previous year or so. The timing of the declaration of war was also important. By 1939 both countries felt that their economies could now withstand a long war and formally offered guarantees to Poland in March.

Hitler had confidently expected no reaction from the Allies after German forces entered Poland. When he received the British ultimatum he was clearly taken aback. Looking rather worried he turned to his entourage and said 'What are we going to do now?'

3. Hitler Told Everybody His War Aims ... but Few People Were Listening

Hitler set out his blueprint for power in his book *Mein Kampf* ('My Struggle'), which was published in 1925. After coming to office Hitler regretted having written the book and said that if in 1924 he had known that he would become Chancellor of Germany, he would never have written it. However, he need not have worried too much. During most of the 1920s he was not taken seriously, as at this time he was a relatively unknown and obscure politician. In 1928 he wrote a second volume of *Mein Kampf*. Even in 1933 when over a million copies of his book had already been sold (and incidentally had made him a rich man) most people complained that it was unreadable as it was so turgid and crudely written. Many of those who did know its contents believed it to be too fanciful and preposterous to be credible ... until it was too late.

It is not surprising that people found the book unreadable as its contents were nothing more than the rantings of a megalomaniac. Hitler outlined his racial theories, which are, alas, so familiar to us today. The Germans (along with the Scandinavians and British) were part of the Aryan race, which was physically and intellectually superior to all other races according to Hitler. It was the giver of modern civilisation. Jews were inferior parasites and were part of an international conspiracy and had to be removed from German soil. Furthermore, Jews (and socialists) had betrayed Germany at the end of the First World War and were responsible for Germany having the hateful Versailles Treaty imposed upon her. The Slavic races of Eastern Europe were also deemed inferior. The subject people of these areas – Poles, Ukrainians and Russians – would be enslaved for the benefit of the German people who needed 'living space' (*lebensraum*).

Incredibly, by the end of 1939 much of his plans had already come to fruition. The Versailles Treaty was clearly dead in the water and nearly all Germans had been united into the Third Reich. However, one part of his plan had not worked out properly. He had hoped that Britain, as a fellow Aryan nation who he claimed to admire, would be on his side. Instead he found himself at war with the country. Nevertheless, he still hoped that the British would see sense and make peace. Two years later with the invasion of the Soviet Union Hitler almost achieved his dream, but found out that the Soviet people were not so inferior after all. If that part also hadn't worked out, his scheme to remove all Jews from Germany became reality and turned into something far more horrific as it extended to most of Europe and transformed itself into the Holocaust.

The demonic dreams of one man led to the deaths of over 40 million people in Europe in the Second World War. It is one of the great tragedies of history that so few people bothered to read that boring tome.

4. Admiral Sir Reginald Aylmer Ranfurly Plunkett-Ernle-Erle-Drax Fails to Cut the Mustard

After Hitler had dealt with Czechoslovakia in March 1939 the next target was clearly Poland.

Hitler was bent on the total destruction of the Polish state, which had been resurrected under the hated Treaty of Versailles. This new state had been given access to the sea through the Polish Corridor, with the result that East Prussia was sundered from the Reich. It was Germany's greatest humiliation.

The problem for Hitler was that he faced a possible war on two fronts if both the Allies and the Soviet Union should intervene. After going back on his promise over Czechoslovakia the chances of getting a deal with the Allies looked bleak. Coming to an understanding with Josef Stalin, the Soviet leader, looked like the only chance. The problem was that the Soviet Union was communist and the arch-enemy of Nazi Germany. They were at opposite ends of the political spectrum and it seemed inconceivable that the two could even get to be on speaking terms.

Stalin, however, observed the situation with an open mind. His primary concern was security of his frontier and he was prepared to make a pact with the highest bidder – whoever it was! The Allies clearly had an opportunity here to bring in the support of Stalin and stop Hitler in his tracks. Chamberlain, however, had a strong distaste for communism and the Soviet Union, and his approach proved somewhat half-hearted. Rather than flying in a high-powered negotiating team to meet Stalin, he instead sent a low-level delegation by slow steamship to Leningrad. The Anglo-French team eventually arrived by train in Moscow in mid-August. The British side was led by Admiral Sir Reginald Aylmer Ranfurly Plunkett-Ernle-Erle-Drax, whose main claim to fame was a handbook on solar heating. The Allied delegation had little to offer the Soviets, however, and Stalin was singularly unimpressed by their inability to negotiate any point without referring back to London and Paris. 'Enough of these games!' exclaimed the Soviet leader.

Germany, on the other hand, offered Stalin everything he wanted. Hitler despatched his Foreign Minister, Joachim von Ribbentrop, to Moscow and there he rapidly agreed the infamous Nazi-Soviet Pact. A vertical line was drawn on the map of Eastern Europe, which delineated the zones of control. Stalin would be allowed to take control of everything east of the line, which included the Baltic States. Poland would be partitioned between the two countries. The Soviet dictator was delighted. He had got the security he wanted as Sovietised Poland would act as a handy buffer zone between himself and Nazi Germany. In addition, he could now sit back and enjoy the spectre of the capitalist powers of Germany, Britain and France battling it out among themselves in a long, mutually destructive conflict.

The Allies were dumbstruck by the deal. They had been outmanoeuvred and could only watch in horror as the two ugly sisters set about the dismemberment of Poland.

5. BRITAIN AND FRANCE ENTER THE PHONEY WAR ... AND AWAIT EVENTS

You may think that the Allies had a chance now to make an early assault on Germany's western frontier while the majority of Hitler's forces were in the east overrunning Poland. But not a bit of it. Instead the Allies did little and sat back. This became known as the Phoney War.

There were reasons for this. France, which had a huge army at its disposal, was locked into a defensive mode. As mentioned before, France hoped to avoid the suffering it had experienced in the First World War of 1914–18. It preferred to hunker down in the Maginot Line and await events. Britain, not unnaturally, followed France's lead on military policy. Cynics might also point out that the laid-back approach was because both prime ministers, Neville Chamberlain for Britain and Edouard Daladier for France, had been the architects of appeasement. They were unlikely to be militarily proactive.

There was also a still lingering hope that Hitler could be persuaded to come to his senses and full-scale war could be avoided. In October and November Hitler even offered peace terms, but nothing came of them. The Allied leaders thought that perhaps economic blockade would lead Hitler to negotiate, but the months passed without result.

If the Allies weren't prepared to launch a direct overland offensive then aerial attack was surely an alternative. However, there was a fear that if the bombers were unleashed complete and utter destruction of Europe's cities would result in massive loss of life. To avoid this perceived horror Britain instead decided to drop 2 million propaganda leaflets over German cities ... with little effect.

The problem with sitting back and waiting on events is that you tend to allow your enemy the initiative. Furthermore, the Maginot Line, alas, had one major problem: it was not complete. The final section along the border with Belgium had never been built and it was obvious to all that a German attack would pass this way. When this event occurred the Allied plan was to advance their armies into Belgium and dig in. However, when exactly the attack would come and where was unclear.

Nevertheless, the Allies were soon given an inkling of Hitler's plans. One foggy morning in January 1940 a small German aircraft was forced to land in Michelen-sur-Meuse in Belgium. The plane contained a German staff officer who was carrying the complete plans for Operation Yellow – Hitler's plan of attack in the West. The officer desperately tried to destroy them but was too late. The Allied commanders, though, thought the documents were a deception and didn't alter their own plans. The Germans did, however, and delayed their offensive.

On 4 April 1940, as German forces massed for Hitler's offensive in the West, Chamberlain made a speech in Central Hall, Westminster. He made a comment that he was soon to regret and would rank alongside his 'Peace in Our Time' statement. With reference to Hitler he said, 'One thing is certain – he has certainly missed the bus.'

6. CAPTAIN HANS LANGSDORFF SCUTTLES HIS SHIP

If during the early stages of the war in Western Europe there was little happening on land, there was certainly some action at sea. By the end of 1939 Britain had already lost 422,000 tons of shipping, mostly due to mines and U-boat activity. In addition, Hitler had sent out his pocket battleship *Admiral Graf Spee* to go commerce raiding in the Atlantic and Indian oceans.

The *Graf Spee* was commanded by Captain Hans Langsdorff. His successful spree of merchant ship sinkings was naturally attracting the attention of the British Royal Navy, who were intent on tracking him down. However, the German battleship was not to be trifled with. It had six fearsome 11-inch guns, which outclassed many of the ships in the Allied fleets. Eventually, three cruisers under the command of Commodore Harewood bravely confronted Langsdorff off the Uruguayan coast in what became known as the Battle of the River Plate.

On paper the British cruisers were hardly a match for the *Graf Spee*. The largest British cruiser in the squadron, HMS *Exeter*, only possessed 8-inch guns and the other two light cruisers, HMS *Ajax* and HMS *Achilles*, were even less well equipped. With its radar-assisted guns the German ship soon scored several punishing hits on the *Exeter* and *Ajax*. Although severely damaged with several members of their crews killed, both ships managed to continue in the fight. More importantly, the German ship was running short of ammunition and enough damage had been inflicted to force her to retreat into Montevideo for important repairs.

After having released his British prisoners and burying his dead Langsdorff had to decide what to do next. It would be some time before he could set sail again and he gleaned from BBC news reports that the aircraft carrier HMS *Ark Royal* and the battle cruiser HMS *Renown* were fast approaching. Little did he realise that this was a British exercise in disinformation and that these British ships were in fact nearly 3,000 miles away. However, rather than risk the lives of his crew by trying to break through the blockade and escape to Argentina, the captain decided there was only one thing to do in this situation and that was to scuttle his ship.

On 17 December 1939, just before dusk, Langsdorff sailed the *Graf Spee* out to the entrance of Montevideo harbour. Twenty-thousand spectators lined the shore and watched the spectacular explosions. Millions around the world also listened to them on the radio. It was a humiliation deeply felt by Langsdorff, who committed suicide three days later.

It marked the first important victory for the British at sea and had been achieved through a simple bluff. The British had, however, been amazed by the accuracy of the German ship's guns and two years later managed to salvage the *Graf Spee's* radar range finder, which was used for further research. Part of the *Graf Spee* can still be seen from Montevideo harbour to this day.

7. THE NORWEGIAN CAMPAIGN IS NOT SO GLORIOUS

As soon as war broke out in September 1939 Winston Churchill was appointed First Lord of the Admiralty. His fertile mind came up with a proposal that would further tighten the blockade the Allies were trying to impose on Germany. The idea was to land forces in Norway, which would then attack neutral Sweden and thereby cut off Germany's vital iron ore supplies. By a quirk of fate, the Germans had also realised the strategic importance of Scandinavia and enemy forces arrived in Norway the day before the British ones!

The Royal Navy was too late to stop the embarkation of numerous well-equipped German troops on 9 April, but was able to strike a surprise blow against the German fleet trapped in Narvik harbour in the north. As many as ten German destroyers, various merchant ships and a U-boat found their way to the bottom of the sea. Hitler would later come to rue these losses when contemplating the invasion of England.

The Allies now changed their plan and decided to support Norwegian resistance by landing their own forces in Trondheim and Narvik. Once ashore, however, Allied troops proved inadequate to the task. In general, they were poorly trained and unprepared for the mountainous and snowy conditions. The highly motivated and very well-prepared German forces pushed the Allied forces back. By 9 June the last Allied troops had been forced to re-embark and leave Norwegian shores. Such evacuations were soon to become an all too familiar sight. It was a humiliating departure.

Unfortunately, worse was to follow. The British aircraft carrier HMS *Glorious* had just been involved in successfully extricating British planes from Norway and was confidently sailing for home. Alas, the captain of the ship had failed to send out spotter planes and was unaware of the approach of the huge twin German battleships *Scharnhorst* and *Gneisenau*. The British ship was no match for these maritime heavyweights and within a short space of time the *Glorious*, together with her escort ships *Acasta* and *Ardent*, were sunk without trace. The story goes that the gallant captain of the *Glorious* stood on the deck as she went down, lit a cigarette, waved and bid the survivors 'Goodbye and good luck!'

It could be said that the Norwegian campaign had turned into something of a fiasco. From the beginning it had been dogged by bad luck and thereafter it been accompanied by incompetence and poor planning. Worse still the Allied troops had been completely outclassed. The one glimmer of light had been the British naval success at the outset.

In retrospect, you may think that Churchill – who after all had cooked up the plan – would have been held directly responsible and compelled to leave office. However, instead Prime Minister Neville Chamberlain was seen by many in the country as being directly responsible for Britain's general lacklustre performance. Events had moved fast. Already on 10 May, under pressure from Parliament, Chamberlain had resigned and had been succeeded by Winston Churchill.

8. CHURCHILL WAS AN ECCENTRIC MAVERICK WHO MADE IT

Although Winston Churchill had a long and illustrious career, it was by no means inevitable that he would become prime minister. Born into an aristocratic family, he did start life with some advantages. He was highly ambitious and served in the army in India and Sudan but made his name in the Boer War where he was captured for a short while before making a daring escape. Off the back of this he entered politics as a Tory MP in 1900, but by 1905 he had switched horses and joined a radical reforming Liberal government where he rather surprisingly helped kick-start the welfare state.

The First World War was a time of mixed fortunes for Churchill. When war broke out in 1914 he held the position of First Lord of the Admiralty. However, his plan to knock Turkey out of the war finished in the Gallipoli debacle of 1915 and he was forced to resign. This left a cloud over him, which lingered in people's memories.

By 1922 the Liberal Party was divided and in decline, and Churchill decided to once again change horses and return to the Tory fold. No other politician in history has changed parties twice and this led to charges that he lacked principle. Amazingly, he was almost immediately given the exalted position of Chancellor of the Exchequer in the next Conservative government (1924–29) but thereafter found himself excluded from office. The 1930s then turned into the 'wilderness years' for Churchill when he seemed out of tune with the times. However, his strident opposition to the policy of appeasement with Hitler meant that in 1939 he was once again in government as First Lord of the Admiralty.

In 1940 many Conservatives opposed his appointment as Prime Minister, but in the end he was the only man for the job. Those doubters would have had their worries confirmed if they had known about his eccentric lifestyle.

Churchill certainly enjoyed strong beverages during the day and especially with meals. He was also what one might describe as a night owl, preferring to work and socialise late into the night. In the mornings he often opted to stay in bed and work. Any visitors, including government ministers, would be expected to conduct important government business there. In later years his visitors would not have been alone in the room as Churchill had his special companions. These were Toby, the budgerigar, and his cat. The cat would often be found at the end of the bed or nestled beside him. Toby also had the run of the room, which was not so amusing. It is recorded that one morning the Chancellor of the Exchequer called in at Chequers to go over some budget papers. At the end of the meeting it was noted by Churchill's private secretary that he had fourteen budgie droppings on his bald pate.

But for the outbreak of war in 1939 Churchill would have remained almost a footnote in history. Life is full of surprises!

9. British Military Writer Invents the *Blitzkrieg* for the Germans

During the 1920s and 1930s various military theorists in Britain looked at why the First World War had been so costly in lives and how war in the future would be different. One writer by the name of Captain B. H. Liddell Hart became particularly influential, not just in Britain but also, more importantly, in Germany. Ironically, these ideas formed the basis of the German military theory of *Blitzkrieg*, which was to be used against Britain's own forces in France and North Africa.

Liddell Hart's thesis was that frontal attacks by infantry on enemy entrenched positions always resulted in heavy losses and was to be avoided at all costs. The next war should avoid this through the use of the tank, which could be employed to break through or get behind enemy positions. It would be a war of mobility where infantry and artillery would also be mechanized and be used in close support of the tanks. Warfare tactics could be flexible and it would be a war of quick manoeuvres designed to keep the enemy off balance.

Many top German generals who took part in the Second World War were inspired by Liddell Hart's book *The British Way in Warfare*, which was translated and read avidly. The German general staff used his ideas to develop their own theory of warfare. *Blitzkrieg* involved the use of tanks, infantry, artillery and dive bombers against one focal point in the enemy line. Once a breakthrough had been achieved, the attacking forces could fan out and the enemy position would eventually collapse. It was a devastating new tactic that was soon to take Europe by storm.

Unfortunately, the British and French military leaders of the 1930s failed to adopt Liddell Hart's central ideas.

France's generals were consumed with the idea of a defensive war and didn't fully realise how effectively the tank could be deployed and how it could change the nature of modern warfare. Indeed, in France in 1940 both Allied armies tended to use tanks in penny packets unsupported by other units. Their impact was thus limited as they soon became isolated in enemy territory.

German commanders, however, soon became masters of the art. The war in Poland in 1939 gave them the opportunity to refine their tactics. In France, after the breakthrough at Sedan, General Erwin Rommel shocked the Allies with the speed of his advance to the coast. Later on, as the Desert Fox, Rommel confounded the British again with his skilful use of tank formations. In 1941–42 generals Heinz Guderian and Erich von Manstein showed their prowess with the technique by ensnaring huge Soviet armies in the vast expanses of Russia and the Ukraine. After 1943, though, the Germans were hoisted with their own petard as Russian commanders learned the trick and started to roll back the Nazi invader.

Ultimately, all the Allied countries, Britain, France and the Soviet Union, had been too slow to understand the changing nature of warfare. They paid a heavy price.

10. The Maginot Line Didn't Defend France

France had suffered horribly in the First World War. Around 1 ½ million Frenchmen had given their lives to defend France. In addition, France had been devastated economically with around 7 million acres of land left ruined due to the trench war fought on its soil. The French authorities decided that rather than suffer a repeat performance, it would build a massive, heavily fortified structure along the border with Germany. It may not keep the Germans out for ever but it did give time for reinforcements to be called up.

The Maginot Line was named after Andre Maginot, the French Minister of War from 1928–32 and was mostly completed by 1939. In actual fact the line ran from Luxembourg all the way down along the Swiss border. At the time it was considered a state-of-the-art construction and designed to be impervious to attack. Interestingly, its name suggests a rather thin linear construction, but was in fact 12 to 16 miles in depth. It was composed of machine-gun outposts, blockhouses and bunkers as well as tank obstacles. It also had air conditioning and an underground railway line ran along its length. It was a monument to French military thinking at the time, which was one of static defence. It is difficult to imagine that France, having built the line, would now engage in any offensive action against Germany.

Despite the massive cost involved in building the line, its main purpose, however, was as a deterrent. The line did not go all the way up to the English Channel but in fact stopped at the Belgian frontier. The reason for this was that at the time of construction the Belgians had been an ally of France and so it would have been counter-productive to have built the line up to the coast.

Despite the Belgians declaring neutrality in 1936, it was still obvious to all that any future attack from Germany could only come through Belgium. Any direct assault on the Maginot would only result in grievous losses for the attacker. In anticipation of any German offensive French military planners intended placing a large number of their forces along the Franco-Belgian frontier.

When the war did commence the inadequacies of the line became evident. French generals had previously decreed that it was not necessary to extend the line opposite the Ardennes forest as it was impenetrable. Alas, it soon became clear that this was exactly where the main German attack was coming from and Allied positions were soon compromised. In the initial offensive only one part of the line at Sedan was overrun by the Germans but the rest was untouched. By the beginning of June 1940 German forces had penetrated deep into French territory leaving the line isolated from the rest of France and irrelevant to the conflict. At the end of the war with Germany the line lay largely intact – a huge useless white elephant.

11. FRENCH GENERALS AND THEIR MEN WERE NOT FIT FOR PURPOSE

By the spring of 1940 the Allies felt more or less ready for a conflict with Germany whenever it should come. The French had a large and well-equipped army, which on paper was formidable enough and roughly on a par in size to the German one. In addition, Britain had sent out its own army called the British Expeditionary Force (BEF) to give support to the French on the Franco-Belgian border. The British having a smaller force went along with French strategy and dispositions. The problem was that on arrival British generals weren't entirely pleased with what they observed in the French Army.

It's often a good idea to have skilled, experienced generals to lead an army. However, it is not particularly good to have elderly commanders who are well passed their best and are, moreover, unsuited to high command. Let me give examples of what I mean. Firstly, there was General Maurice Gamelin, Commander-in-Chief of all Allied forces. He was sixty-seven and clearly out of his depth. He was generally described as small, quiet and singularly lacking in vigour and charisma. More importantly, he possessed a distinct inability to give any clear orders. His deputy was no better. General Alphonse Georges was Commander-in-Chief for the North-East Front. He had been severely wounded in the 1934 assassination of King Alexander of Yugoslavia in Marseilles. Thereafter Georges had remained something of a physical and psychological wreck, who had great difficulty keeping cool in a crisis. A further unfortunate fact was that these two generals were barely on speaking terms – just the sort of chaps you need, then, to galvanise your troops as German tanks appear on the horizon.

Gamelin and Georges were fatally wedded to strategies of the First World War. The Allied and German forces, they believed, would once more fight each other in trenches. The Maginot Line would protect France in the south. Along the unprotected North-East Front with Belgium, though, the concept was one of a long line with tanks interspersed in small groups. Allied forces would advance into Belgium and dig in when hostilities began. There appeared to be little acknowledgement that the next war would be one of movement and manoeuvre. Indeed, the most frightening aspect of French dispositions was that almost all their forces were committed to the front line with virtually none in reserve. There was no plan B should the Germans break through the line.

If the generals did not inspire confidence French soldiers inspired even less. British generals were horrified with their slovenliness. In November 1939 General Alan Brooke visited French General Corap's 9th Army, which was stationed just north of Sedan. He noted that the French soldiers were unshaven with the horses ungroomed and they showed a general lack of pride. He went on to say, 'What shook me most however was the look in the men's faces, their disgruntled and insubordinate looks… '

Sedan was to be the site of the German breakthrough.

12. The British Did Not Really Betray the French at Dunkirk

This statement is not really true, although it is a controversial view held by many. The truth is that at times British general staff did not keep their French allies completely informed of their intentions. However, there were reasons for this. During the headlong retreat communications were not always easy and all too often the whereabouts of French and British commanders was not known. Sometimes relations were indeed rather frosty between Allied commanders. More importantly some messages were not passed on correctly leading to misunderstandings.

The German offensive commenced on 10 May 1940. Upon receiving the information that German units were advancing into Holland, Allied armies immediately moved into Belgium, as planned, and dug in along the River Dyle. However, hardly had they done this when news reached French and British commanders that German panzers had already crossed the River Meuse at Sedan. The French commander, Gamelin, had placed inadequate forces there believing the Ardennes forest to be impenetrable. With no reserves to confront them the Germans were able to advance rapidly. It soon became obvious that the BEF and other French forces in Belgium had fallen into a trap. By 20 May Heinz Guderian's 2nd Panzer division had reached the sea near Abbeville cutting the Allied armies off from the rest of France. French attempts at a counter-attack against the armoured thrust proved desultory.

By 25 May Lord Gort, the British general in charge of the BEF, decided to call off his own counter-attack and head for Dunkirk, the only available port on the French coast. The intention was to evacuate the BEF. It was now that confusion about British intentions came about. Although Winston Churchill made it clear to his French counterpart that the British were intent on evacuation, this message was not passed on to French commanders. Some French generals believed that the British were pulling back in order to create a fortified position into which Allied forces could retreat. In the end it was more about poor communication than betrayal.

British generals, on the other hand, had every right to feel that they themselves had been let down. Too many French units were subject to low morale and defeatism and disintegrated before the German advance. Nevertheless, by 30 May substantial numbers of French and British troops were able to retreat back behind a perimeter around Dunkirk.

Irrespective of nationality, Allied soldiers were taken on board by all the British vessels that participated in the evacuation. By the night of 2–3 June all BEF forces had been evacuated but Churchill insisted that the Royal Navy and the myriad of smaller vessels should go back once more to pick up the remaining French troops left on the beaches. In the end, although 40,000 Frenchmen were taken prisoner at Dunkirk, 120,000 were evacuated to Britain. In addition, all high-ranking French generals were taken to safety.

Admiral Jean Abrial, the overall French commander at Dunkirk, described the British effort as '*magnifique*'.

13. Hitler Spares the British Army

One of the great mysteries of the Second World War is why Hitler did not make the most of his opportunity in May and June 1940 to destroy the British forces that found themselves surrounded at Dunkirk. A myth has grown up that the Führer wanted to negotiate peace terms with the British and so held back his panzers in the hope that the British would come to him begging for clemency. The surprise is that there is no evidence from historians to support this hypothesis.

In truth it is most likely that the great all-seeing, all-knowing dictator was nervous and fearful that his forces were overextended. In the campaign against France he tended to defer to his generals, in particular Gerd von Rundstedt, the commander of Army Group A. This unit had burst through at Sedan and driven a wedge between the allied armies in northern France. Hitler and his commanders became concerned that the German panzers risked becoming isolated as they raced ahead and left the infantry behind. As a result of this there were several 'halt' orders as the German high command sought to rein in their wayward tank commanders. These orders gave the British BEF commander, Lord Gort, vital time to extricate his forces.

The final halt order on 24 May gave the British a further forty-eight hours to reinforce the Dunkirk perimeter. Hitler now further compounded his error by declaring that the land around Dunkirk was not suitable for tanks as it was too marshy and full of canals. The infantry and the air force (Luftwaffe) led by Hermann Goering would finish the job. His panzer generals were furious as they saw an easy victory slipping through their fingers. Nevertheless, the German leadership still confidently expected a huge Allied army to fall into their hands.

All this provided the British with time to commence 'Operation Dynamo' – the code name for the evacuation of troops from Dunkirk, which began on 26 May. A vast armada of 860 vessels was mobilised to save the beleaguered forces stranded on the beaches. Taking part were over 200 Royal Navy ships and hundreds of civilian craft including liners, pleasure steamers, barges, trawlers, ferries and yachts. By 4 June, despite facing the gauntlet of constant Luftwaffe and U-boat attacks, the bulk of the BEF had been shipped back to Britain and safety. Although they lost all their equipment and 65,000 vehicles, the soldiers of the BEF would soon be redeployed to carry on the struggle.

Hitler had expected an easy victory at Dunkirk. The fact that the BEF escaped was not due to any negotiating ploy but poor generalship. The British people heaved a collective sigh of relief and evoked the 'Dunkirk spirit'. Winston Churchill described it as 'a miracle of deliverance'. For Hitler it turned into something approaching a disaster. He did indeed hope that Britain would agree to peace terms. His failure to force Britain to the negotiating table meant that ultimately he was to end up with a war on two fronts.

14. Hitler Rubs Salt in the Wound at Compiègne

After the surprise German breakthrough at Sedan, France's top commanders, generals Gamelin and Georges, collapsed into tears and despondency. Further bad news followed with the British retreat and escape at Dunkirk. Now the might of the *Wehrmacht* (German armed forces) was turned on the rest of France. German forces cut through the French Army at such speed that even the Germans themselves were astounded. By 14 June Hitler's troops entered a rather desolate and empty Paris and four days later the French government asked for an armistice. It had taken only six weeks for Germany to lay waste that once great power.

The Nazi dictator performed a little jig on hearing the news of France's capitulation. It was a victory to savour. Twenty-two years earlier at the end of the long and bitter conflict of the First World War it was Germany that had had to ask for an armistice. After four years of horrific trench warfare Germany had lost and the Allies had forced her to sign the hated Treaty of Versailles. Now France would be made to pay for that humiliation.

Under Hitler's terms three-fifths of France (in the north and west) would come directly under German occupation. The rump of France in the south would become Vichy France and a vassal of the Third Reich. French leaders signed the surrender at Compiègne in the very same railway carriage that Germany had signed the Armistice in 1918.

For the French it was a poignant reminder of their sad reversal of fortune.

15. A Scarlet Pimpernel Helps the Allied Cause

A rather bedraggled and unshaven individual was ushered into the office of Harold Macmillan, a future prime minister, but at that time a junior minister in Churchill's government. The man in question had just escaped from war-torn France and he had a remarkable story to tell. It was Charles Howard, the 20th Earl of Suffolk.

The earl was an extraordinary character whose life was surrounded by legends and stories of derring-do, which often turned out to be true. To his friends he was known as 'wild Jack' Howard and he sported a pair of guns, which he named Oscar and Genevieve.

Charles Howard was born into one of the finest noble families in England. His mother was the daughter of one of the richest men in America, the founder of the Marshall Field department store. However, Charles decided not to follow the usual route of a young nobleman. Instead he married an actress and went off to the University of Edinburgh where he immersed himself in science. In early 1940, at the age of thirty-three, he was appointed as the British government's liaison officer with France's Armament's Ministry in Paris.

By the beginning of June the situation in Paris was becoming critical. Many in the French government were clearing their offices and heading for Bordeaux. On 10 June Charles Howard joined them but not before he had assembled thirty-three top scientists to accompany him. With him also were a colleague and their two secretaries. On arrival at Bordeaux the situation was chaotic, but eventually he found a British tramp named SS *Broomhead*, which was rescuing refugees at the time.

It soon became clear that the 20th Earl had been organising much more than just these scientists. After a while two notable physicists arrived by the names of Hans van Halben and Frédéric Joliot-Curie. Together they had been doing top-secret research on nuclear fusion. With them came 52 gallons of heavy water that had been extricated from Norway and which the Germans would have dearly liked to get their hands on to create their own nuclear bomb. Also on the quayside were 600 tons of valuable machine tools and the managing director of the Antwerp Diamond Bank, who carried with him a parcel containing gem diamonds worth £400 million in today's terms.

At first the French government would not allow the earl to escape with such a cargo. Only after he had personally berated France's new prime minister, Marshall Petain, was he given the go-ahead. Several days later the vessel arrived safely back in British shores. Herbert Morrison, a British government minister, later recorded 'A considerable service has been rendered to the Allied cause by the safe arrival of this shipload.'

After this the intrepid earl set about defusing bombs during the Blitz. He successfully dealt with thirty-four bombs but, sadly, a booby-trapped one killed him and his team in May 1941.

The earl deserves the title of the Scarlet Pimpernel of the Second World War.

16. MUSSOLINI EXPECTS EASY PICKINGS BUT GETS SOME NASTY SHOCKS INSTEAD

Adolf Hitler was not the only dictator who harboured great imperial pretensions at this time. His Italian ally and fellow dictator Benito Mussolini wanted to carve out a vast empire encompassing large parts of the Mediterranean and Africa. He saw himself as some kind of reincarnated Caesar creating a new Roman empire.

Mussolini's direction of foreign policy, however, was less that of a great general or a shrewd statesman but rather one that was more akin to an opportunistic vulture. Italy had already previously gained a colonial empire but from 1935 *Il Duce* was set upon acquiring new territory. In 1935 he had launched the invasion of Ethiopia and in May 1939 he had seized Albania forcing the flight of King Zog. These had been easy victories achieved over vastly inferior forces.

Believing that Britain and France were the two main countries that were likely to thwart him in his ambitions he had teamed up with Hitler in the Rome-Berlin Axis in 1936. This had been further strengthened into a military alliance in the Pact of Steel in May 1939. Mussolini ignored those around him who warned that tying himself to Hitler would lead to disaster.

At the beginning of the war it seemed that the Italian dictator had indeed backed the right horse. Hitler had easily despatched Poland and when France seemed to be on the point of defeat, Mussolini decided to seize his moment. On 10 June 1940 he stood on a balcony in Piazza Venezia in Rome and made a fateful speech. In his usual oratorical style he folded his arms and rolled his eyes and declared that Italy was now at war with the Allies.

Italian forces immediately attacked France and Mussolini was rewarded with some small pieces of French territory. In September, believing the British to be virtually defeated, he decided to send 250,000 troops into Egypt from the neighbouring Italian colony of Libya. Instead of advancing on the Suez Canal directly, however, his forces were told to halt 65 miles from Cairo and await further orders. The weaknesses of the Italian Army soon became apparent. Poorly equipped and trained and suffering from low morale, they all too quickly succumbed to a smaller British force. Within two months 130,000 Italian prisoners had been taken and the British were at the gates of Tripoli, the Libyan capital. It had been a catastrophic reversal.

In October the dictator had also attacked Greece hoping for an easy victory. Italian forces moved forward from Albania but in the mountainous and wintry conditions the Greeks were able to put up valiant resistance. Embarrassingly, the Duce's troops soon found themselves pushed back into Albania in an ignominious retreat. It was at this moment, however, that Hitler decided to send in German forces to North Africa and the Balkans to save his feckless friend.

Mussolini's great imperial pretensions had rapidly turned into farce. His fate and that of his country was now in the hands of his Nazi ally.

17. Hitler Hopes for Peace with Britain

After the fall of France in June 1940 the German dictator hoped that Britain would quickly see her position was hopeless and come to terms. For Hitler Britain was the wrong enemy anyway. Ideologically, Britain was a fellow Anglo-Saxon power with whom he wanted to divide up the world. He admired Britain, with her vast empire, and was prepared to let the British keep it intact. In exchange he expected Britain to allow him a free hand in Europe. It could only be a matter of time before the British came to their senses.

Indeed, to begin with, he took time out hoping that the British would get in touch. He toured Paris and then returned to his mountain retreat and awaited events. Some early indiscretions by British diplomats hinting that Britain was ready to negotiate only encouraged Hitler in his thinking. However, back in Britain Churchill and his cabinet were adamant that any talks with Hitler would only be from a position of weakness leading to a humiliating peace settlement. It was better to struggle on. After all, Britain still had a strong navy and air force and any invasion attempt by the Germans would be fraught with difficulty. However, the British Army was severely weakened after Dunkirk and it was unclear if a determined Nazi onslaught could actually be held back.

On 19 July 1940 Hitler had had enough of waiting. He had received no offers of peace from the British and so he set out his stall in a speech to the Reichstag (German parliament). As a magnanimous conqueror he was prepared to offer a peace deal, but if the British continued in the war then he would have no alternative but to destroy her empire. Hitler and his entourage were incredulous when the offer was rebuffed almost out of hand.

The Nazi dictator now knew that he had to take the war to the British mainland in order to force a settlement. He had already given a directive for 'Operation Sea Lion', which was for an invasion of Britain if all else failed. It required air supremacy and secure passage for the invasion fleet across the English Channel. However, Hitler hoped that invasion would be unnecessary. He envisaged that the superior German Air Force together with the U-boats lurking in the seas around Britain would be able to bludgeon and so strangle the perfidious British so that they would come begging for peace terms.

Fortunately for the British events did not go according to plan. The British fighter force proved a worthy foe to the Luftwaffe and so Hitler was never able to secure the right conditions for 'Operation Sea Lion'. By September 1940 the Führer had scrapped his ideas for invasion.

By this time the Nazi warlord had already turned his attention east towards the Soviet Union.

18. THE GERMAN AIR FORCE GETS ITS COMEUPPANCE

One of the rather surprising aspects of the Battle of Britain is the initial view each side had of their opponent's capabilities. Hitler had given the German pilots the task of establishing air supremacy prior to invasion. They were fresh from victories over Poland and France and believed that the British air force would be no match for them. They expected their opposite numbers to be very inexperienced and the numbers of planes and pilots to be low. Confidence was sky-high! On the other hand, British air intelligence vastly overestimated the strength of the Luftwaffe and its efficiency. Both sides were wrong.

Perhaps this last statement should be qualified. British pilots were initially much less experienced on the whole than their opponents. However, they had time to practise in the two months while Hitler dithered after the fall of France. The respective size of the air forces was an issue that proved decisive. The British believed the Germans had around 7,000 fighter planes. The truth was far different. In fact, the Germans only had 1,011 operational fighters in August 1940, which was slightly fewer than the British! Furthermore, despite the British suffering higher losses during the battle, they easily out-produced the supposedly efficient Third Reich. The reality was that Hitler's Germany was very chaotic and German fighter production was relatively low. During the months of June to October 1940, the Nazi state was only able to turn out 919 ME 109 fighter planes whereas British factories managed to get over 2,000 Hurricanes and Spitfires into the front line. So you can see that Winston Churchill's famous speech about 'the few' should in fact refer to the Germans.

German fighter pilots soon found out that they were not the overwhelming favourites to win as they had expected. Although the ME109 was a superb plane at the forefront of technology it, performed less well at lower altitudes, although at 30,000 feet it was unmatched in its performance. The pilots of the British Hawker Hurricane and the Spitfire on the other hand found that while they were hampered at the higher altitudes, they could actually out turn their opponents at 20,000 feet. Unfortunately for German pilots, the Head of the Luftwaffe, Hermann Goering, understood little about modern aerial warfare and demanded that the fighters accompany the slow, lumbering bombers that flew at the lower altitudes. The idea was that the bombers would be a lure for the British fighters. These strictures, as you can imagine, put German fighters at a severe disadvantage. By the end of October German losses were becoming unacceptably high and it was clear that the RAF was far from being destroyed. Hitler now decided to call off his aerial offensive.

The German fighter pilots had arrogantly expected an easy victory. In the end they found themselves embroiled in a costly war of attrition, which they were clearly losing. Britain would now emerge as a beacon of hope for those enduring Nazi occupation across Europe.

19. Churchill's Speeches Inspired the Nation … Mostly

Winston Churchill's stirring oratory during the Second World War has become part of the collective memory for British people. During the bleakest moments of the war when events had conspired to leave the British alone in Europe, Churchill inspired the British people to struggle on. His speeches were always his own carefully crafted words and never those of a professional writer. For many people at the time who gathered around their radios, his rather grand style would strike a chord in their emotions. His broadcasts were eagerly awaited.

Churchill's speeches are well known and include many memorable phrases. These are some examples. On becoming prime minister in May 1940 he told the people that he had 'nothing to offer but blood, tears, toil and sweat'. Soon after Dunkirk, on 4 June, he addressed the House of Commons with this rousing speech: 'We shall fight on the beaches, we shall fight on the landing-grounds, we shall fight in the fields and in the streets … we shall never surrender.' After the fall of France he rallied the people by telling them that the 'Battle of Britain' was about to begin and that this was to be their 'finest hour'. At the height of the air war over Britain in August 1940 when the RAF was battling for survival, he made a speech that included the line, 'Never in the field of human conflict was so much owed by so many to so few.'

The reason that Churchill's speeches and phrases still resonate is that he was very adept at using classical rhetorical devices. This involved repetition of words and phrases as well as contrasting pairs. He also used short punchy Anglo-Saxon words for maximum effect. Indeed his speeches are masterpieces of the art of speech-making and the sound bite. Before the war many British people thought his speeches were ridiculously grandiose and inappropriate. However, during Britain's darkest hour the rhetoric seemed to suit the mood much more.

Not everybody was enthusiastic about his speeches, however. Churchill often had to deliver some tough messages about the course and duration of the war. People were fearful about what the future held. This meant that people were focusing on the message rather than the lofty words and quite a few listeners were quietly critical. In addition, others felt that during his 'finest hour' speech he was actually drunk, although this may have been due less to the brandy but rather to his slurred pronunciation of the letter 'S'. In the end, more people were less inspired at the time than we like to think.

Strangely, Churchill was rather loath to broadcast the speeches he had already made to the House of Commons. A myth grew up after the war that a Churchill impressionist had recorded them for the radio instead. This is untrue. The radio broadcasts we have today are the genuine Churchill ones and form an important part of the story of the British war effort.

20. The Horror of the Blitz Was Incessant

The Blitz was the period of continual heavy bombing of British cities from September 1940 to May 1941. For Hitler it was a continuation of the Battle of Britain by other means. The aim was to so demoralise the British people and to degrade the infrastructure so drastically that Britain in desperation would sue for terms.

It all started when London was heavily bombed on September 7 1940. It heralded a further fifty-seven successive nights of bombing for the capital. As was to be a common feature the docks and the East End were particularly badly hit. Soon after this, King George VI and Queen Elizabeth were to join in the misery when Buckingham Palace was hit while they were in residence. They afterwards said that at least now 'they could look the East End in the face'. Seeing the plight of bombed-out Londoners reduced Churchill to tears. A further example of the horror was the hit on Balham High Street in October resulting in a London bus falling into a crater created by a massive explosion. A bomb had hit the tube there and water and sewage gushed into the station killing sixty-eight people.

The bombing, however, was not just located in the London area. Hitler was keen to hit ports and industrial centres if he was to undermine Britain's war-making capacity. So Coventry was hit on the nights of 14 and 15 November. The city was so devastated that a new word was coined by the Germans – 'to coventrate'. Among other places hit during the Blitz were Birmingham, Liverpool, Grimsby, Swansea, Bristol, Glasgow and Clydeside. Fortunately for the British, the attacks on sites outside the capital were rarely prosecuted for more than two consecutive nights allowing them to make a fairly rapid recovery and production soon got going again. As the weeks and months passed a defiant spirit grew up and 'We can take it' became a refrain of the period.

The raids actually intensified in the spring of 1941 and 10 May proved to be the worst night of the Blitz for London. Churchill would often view the bombing from the roof of the Air Ministry, much to the dismay of his ministers. However, suddenly the bombing stopped as Hitler turned his attention away towards Eastern Europe.

In order to provide some variety during the Blitz the Germans had utilised an array of bombs. To begin with there were the usual high-explosive bombs. Others in their arsenal were more fearsome, such as the 'Satan' bomb weighing in at 4,000 lb and the Max at 5,500 lb. One of these could create a crater big enough for two double-decker buses! Perhaps most destructive were the magnetic mines dropped by parachute, which on contact with the ground could cause damage scattered over a very wide area.

The grizzly death toll of the Blitz was around 44,000 people with some 71,000 injured. Nevertheless, it was not as devastating as had been feared and Britain struggled on resiliently.

21. The British Lived in Caves

The intensive bombing of the Blitz almost on a daily basis meant many ordinary British citizens were desperate to find secure places to bed down for the night. Londoners had recourse to the underground tube stations. Many others decided to brazen it out in the 'safety' of their own homes with their own forms of bomb shelter. Others still managed to secure protection in the most unexpected ways.

Some, who had a garden, opted for the Anderson shelter. This was created by digging deep into the ground and placing corrugated iron over the top in order to create a sturdy roof. Extra protection was offered by placing turf and soil over it. If you preferred to stay inside your home, however, you could climb into something resembling a metal cage called a Morrison shelter. The hope was that should your dwelling suffer a direct hit, you would have a somewhat better chance of being pulled out alive.

If you didn't favour either of those options you could try to get protection using 'public shelters'. These, for example, could be town halls or railway stations, but these all too often afforded the user little safety. You could, if you were lucky, find peace of mind in the basement of a department store, a railway tunnel or a church crypt.

In London, where possible, people found shelter in the underground stations. At first the government tried to prevent this as they didn't want people living down there on a permanent basis and thereby impeding the running of the transport system. However, in the end, 'people power' won through. The main concern was sanitation and hygiene. Chemical toilets and bunk beds were provided, but conditions remained cramped. As time went by systems were developed to ease the misery.

Platform canteens and tube trains offered such treats as cigarettes, tea, coffee, cakes and buns. People soon started to provide their own entertainment by organising various activities such as parties, quizzes and discussion groups. Others brought along wind-up gramophones. Later educational lectures and classes became available. A high point was reached when ENSA (Entertainments National Service Administration or 'Every Night Something Awful') brought in various entertainers such as George Formby and Shakespearean actors. Films also became available when projectors were imported.

Large numbers of people, however, also resorted to sheltering in caves. Those in Ramsgate in Kent boasted 3 miles of tunnels with space for 60,000 people. The local council had set up an electricity supply with ample seating and bunks. In Dover and Chislehurst the caves were initially more basic. In the latter donkeys were employed to take away the ash bins used as latrines. But later on, as with the underground, conditions became more civilised with dances and singsongs being organised and a cinema provided. There were even shops and a hospital!

So Hitler may have dreamt of bombing the British people back into the Stone Age, but the truth is that only a small minority used caves as temporary shelters.

22. The Italian Fleet Gets a Drubbing

When Benito Mussolini declared war on Britain in June 1940 he believed she was about to surrender and her empire was ripe for dismemberment. This was surely the time to make the Mediterranean an Italian sea, as in the days of ancient Rome. As we have already seen in the Desert War (Fact 16), however, things did not go according to plan. The Italian fleet, though, did pose a greater potential threat for the British in the Mediterranean as the sea represented a vital link to India and their Far Eastern possessions via Egypt and the Suez Canal.

The Italian Navy on paper was quite formidable. It contained six battleships, nineteen cruisers, fifty-four destroyers and various other vessels such as submarines and torpedo boats making a grand total of 262. The British fleet may have dwarfed this but the Royal Navy was spread out across the world patrolling the shores at home, the Atlantic and the seas of the Far East. Fortunately for the British, Mussolini was loath to commit his fleet in a straight battle but preferred to keep it as a 'fleet in being'.

The British did not waste time in asserting their strength. The first blow was struck not in a battle directly with British surface ships but by planes despatched from an aircraft carrier. Admiral Cunningham, Commander-in-Chief in the Mediterranean, moored the carrier *Illustrious* east of the Italian port of Taranto. This base situated in the south-east corner of the Italian peninsula had already been reconnoitred and had revealed itself as home to a large group of Italian battleships. On 11 November 1940 twenty-one Swordfish torpedo bombers lifted off from the British carrier. With little opposition the planes were able to fly in low and release their loads. Three battleships were hit. One, *Cavour*, was sunk and another two were severely damaged. Cunningham had dealt the Italians a severe blow and had reasserted Britain's position of dominance.

In March 1941 the Italian fleet was dealt a further blow when Admiral Cunningham, using decrypts from Bletchley Park, was able to catch up with the Italian fleet west of Crete. The Italian fleet had sallied forth in the hope of disrupting the British operations in the eastern Mediterranean. In an action known as the Battle of Matapan, much of the enemy fleet escaped; however, the British commander was able to sink three fast, heavy cruisers and two destroyers. Such aggressive actions encouraged Mussolini to keep his fleets in ports back at home and out of harm's way.

However, the British Navy did not have it all its own way. The German Luftwaffe, with its bases in Italy and Greece, represented a fearsome weapon inflicting massive losses during the evacuation from Crete in May that year. The situation for the British fleet in the Mediterranean became precarious.

23. The 'Desert Fox' Causes an Upset

In February 1941 Hitler decided that he needed to shore up the desperate position of his ally Mussolini in North Africa. In February 1941 he despatched General Erwin Rommel (the Desert Fox) with a makeshift army dubbed the *Afrika Korps* down to Tripoli. His task was to save the Italian empire in North Africa. British forces there had been within an ace of taking the whole of Libya and pushing the Axis out of North Africa. However, Churchill's sudden decision to switch some of these forces to Greece had forced the British desert army to halt their advance.

General Archibald Wavell, the Commander-in-Chief of British forces in the Middle East, mistakenly believed that Rommel was still awaiting further reinforcements and that his ambitions were limited to only trying to seize Benghazi nearby. Instead Rommel struck immediately with the intention of driving the British back and seizing Egypt itself. The speed and direction of the attack left British forces reeling. Rommel cut across the desert inland and headed for Tobruk further along the coast. In the process he cut off a large number of British forces and embarrassingly even seized two leading British generals. Amazingly, Tobruk held out for over seven months before the British launched a counter-attack with the new Eighth Army. Rommel was forced into a temporary withdrawal, but in January 1942 he once again launched a surprise attack, which sent British forces into a headlong retreat back to a line inside Egypt at El Alamein.

The British would need new generals with fresh ideas if they were to stave off disaster.

24. Operation Barbarossa Kicks In Late

The reader may recall that Hitler had signed a non-aggression pact with the Soviet leader, Josef Stalin, in August 1939 (Fact 4). However, Hitler viewed Communist Russia as his greatest enemy and so war with the great leviathan was inevitable sooner or later. Russia was also part of his ideological goal of gaining 'living space' in the east at the expense of the 'inferior' Slavs. He was not concerned about an undefeated Britain. Once the Soviets were crushed the perfidious Brits, lacking allies, would sue for peace.

In December 1940 Hitler had issued Directive No. 21 for the invasion of the Soviet Union, codenamed Operation Barbarossa. The date set was for 15 May 1941. On paper Stalin had formidable armed forces. But appearances flattered. When Stalin had launched a huge offensive against little Finland in December 1939, Soviet forces had suffered a series of humiliating defeats before eventually prevailing. The Soviet Army was revealed to be very poorly led and equipped. Hitler gleefully commented, 'You only have to kick in the door, and the whole rotten structure will collapse.'

By spring 1941 Hitler had amassed huge forces on the frontier with the Soviet Union. But preparations were not complete and in May he was forced to divert German forces to the Balkans in order to bail out his hapless ally Mussolini.

Finally, later than expected, on June 22 1941, a mighty army of 3 million German troops and 1 million foreign contingents crossed the 1,800-mile Soviet frontier stretching from Finland to the Black Sea.

25. Stalin Wouldn't Believe the Truth

In 1941 Stalin viewed the spectre of war with Nazi Germany with horror. Under the pact with Hitler he believed he had bought himself time to build up his armed forces and his defences while Hitler fought the French and British. But Hitler's rapid victories had laid bare Stalin's policy and the Führer was now able to point his armies eastward. However, the Soviet dictator still clung to the hope that the German war machine would need more time to prepare an attack on the vastness of the Soviet Union.

The Soviet Army was still woefully unprepared for a major conflict. The reason for this could be clearly laid at the feet of Stalin himself. In his usual paranoid and vindictive way he had recently set about removing any threat to his position from inside his own armed forces. In the period 1937–38 he had purged nearly all his top commanders along with 37,000 officers. Although many of these later returned (if they hadn't been shot!), it created chaos and loss of morale just when war with Nazi Germany was in the offing. In addition, the Soviet Union was still especially vulnerable to an attack. Stalin had moved forces forward to the new frontline in Poland, but defences there were far from ready leaving his armies dangerously exposed. Moreover, the old defensive lines along the previous Soviet frontier had been abandoned and no longer offered any security.

Stalin did all he could to keep his Nazi partner satisfied with the pact. The agreement had stipulated that raw materials such as cereals and oil were to be sent to Germany in exchange for military equipment, ships and engines. The Soviet leader made sure his country kept strictly to his side of the bargain.

This was not to be enough, however. In the spring of 1941 it was clear that there was a massive build-up of Nazi forces on the Soviet frontier. Rather than face reality, Stalin tamely accepted the German story that the forces there were merely on manoeuvres. Further information that an offensive was about to take place in late June came from Britain, Japan and inside the German Air Ministry. Stalin refused to believe these sources as they had previously warned of a German offensive in May, but nothing had happened. They had in fact all been right but Hitler had delayed his offensive at the last moment. The Soviet leader also tried to comfort himself with the thought that late June was too late in the year to launch an attack.

Stalin now further added to his woes. Fearful of provoking the Nazi leader he dismissed the need for mobilisation even when it he had clear information the attack was about to commence.

Hitler was thus allowed to gain complete surprise. Soviet forces were left with no prior warning resulting in massive, catastrophic losses. Stalin's foolhardy denial of reality almost led to the destruction of the Soviet Union itself. Lucky circumstance allowed it to survive.

26. HITLER MADE A MISTAKE BY TURNING SOUTH

As mentioned before (Fact 25) Stalin had left his forces unprepared when Hitler's invasion of the Soviet Union was launched. The Germans, once again using their blitzkrieg tactics, made short shrift of Soviet forces facing them. Within a week Nazi forces had reached Minsk in Belorussia and soon ensnared 340,000 enemy soldiers. In the air the German Luftwaffe reigned almost supreme as many Russian planes were destroyed on the ground in the first few hours of 22 June. In fact, around 4,000 planes were lost in the first two weeks alone.

The speed of the advance shook Stalin to the core. At first he retreated in despair to his country dacha but eventually he pulled himself together and took charge. Declaring himself Supreme Commander he set out the strategy to confront the invader. There would be fierce discipline, constant offensives and a 'no retreat' policy. This was a successful policy that had been used in the Russian Civil War in 1918–21, but was hardly appropriate now. The German Army was using vast encircling movements and such a policy only invited further disasters. As testament to Stalin's new discipline General D. Pavlov and his staff were blamed for the failure at Minsk and shot. Other generals who were seen to have 'failed' met a similar fate.

By August Hitler's general staff believed that they could seize the Russian capital and bring about a decisive blow. However, Hitler could see rich pickings in the Southern front in Ukraine. Stalin had mistakenly placed a large part of his armies there and Hitler could see that by diverting his Army Group Centre south he could win a victory of epic proportions. The result was that in a short campaign Hitler's armies bagged over 500,000 Soviet troops. No other country in history had suffered such losses but Stalin's regime nevertheless continued in the war.

It was now that Hitler discovered his error. Belatedly, he turned his attention on Moscow. Leningrad (today's St Petersburg) was already surrounded and it seemed only a matter of time before the capital fell, too. Stalin sent in further scratch forces to hold the line and the people of Moscow came out to dig anti-tank ditches. Although further setbacks followed these measures served to delay the Nazi onslaught. By November the Russian winter closed in with all its traditional severity. With temperatures of -30 degrees Celsius the German juggernaut ground to a halt on the outskirts of Moscow. Lacking winter clothing and with the fuel in their tanks and vehicles frozen over, Hitler's exhausted men were in a perilous state. Stalin now brought in his top general, G. K. Zhukov, to launch a counter-attack with fresh Siberian troops. In a desperate struggle Hitler's front line was thrown back 100 miles and Moscow was saved.

This proved significant. Hitler had failed to achieve a knock-out blow in the first year of campaigning. It was now set to be a lengthy war of attrition in which Germany was unlikely to be the winner.

27. Stalin Was a Brutal Paranoid Dictator

Imagine a European dictatorship in the 1930s and '40s. Opponents of the regime are carted off and face torture, execution or being placed in special camps in which they will be lucky to survive. Millions died in this way. You may think I'm talking about Hitler's Germany, but in fact this is life inside the Soviet Union under the rule of Josef Stalin.

How did it all start? Stalin means 'man of steel' and, of course, wasn't his real name but one he chose for himself later. He was born Joseph Dzhughashvili in the small town of Gori in Georgia in 1878. At first he was set for the priesthood and studied hard at the local seminary where he often received the top grade in nearly all subjects. However, Georgia was under the rule of the Tsars and suddenly in his last year of study he dropped out and adopted the life of a Marxist revolutionary bent on removing their imperialist rule.

Eventually, he reached the attention of Vladimir Lenin, leader of the hard-line Communist or Bolshevik movement in Russia. Lenin appreciated his ability to organise and as a result he rose in the party. Stalin took part in the Communist seizure of power in October 1917 but in the civil war that followed he showed his true colours. At Taritsyn on the River Volga he repressed the local peasants with such ferocity that even some other communists were shocked. The town was later renamed Stalingrad 'in honour' of his time there. He was by now beginning to show his real character – sly, volatile and vindictive.

Lenin died in 1924 without a clear successor. Trotsky, the darling of the party, fancied his chances, but Stalin had taken control of the party apparatus and slowly removed him from the centre of power. Trotsky, fearing for his life, fled abroad.

By 1928 Stalin was in complete control of the Soviet state and nobody was to be trusted. Anybody could be denounced as a counter-revolutionary and be sent to a gulag (labour camp) in Siberia or tortured in Lubyanka prison in Moscow. Even old comrades in the party were purged in a series of show trials and this was followed in 1938 when 90 per cent of the officer class were removed from the army. Later on, Molotov, his Foreign Minister, was forced to denounce his own wife, who ended up in a gulag. Perhaps thirty million people Soviet citizens died in this way in his twenty-five-year rule. One of Stalin's favourite bon mots was, 'one death is a tragedy: one million is a statistic.'

However, when it came to the war with Nazi Germany his rule did have beneficial effects. In the 1930s he had thoroughly modernised the economy and his tight grip on the state meant that Russia did not collapse as it had done in 1917 during the First World War.

Stalin continued as leader until 1953 when he died of natural causes.

28. A British Submarine Keeps a Reindeer on Board!

One of the supposed myths of the war was that a British submarine that was on a visit to Russia in 1941 took a deer on board, which was then accompanied back to England. It seems improbable but it is true – a recently unearthed photograph has confirmed the legend. How and why it came about is rather bizarre, as you might expect.

A British submarine by the name of HMS *Trident* was sent on a goodwill mission to the Soviet Union after the Nazi invasion in June 1941. Her destination was Polyarny, near Murmansk, in the Arctic Circle. However, the submarine's main mission was to attack German vessels off the Norwegian coast. In August, after a tour of duty, the submarine returned to Polyarny for much-needed repairs. It was then that the unexpected occurred.

Prior to the British submarine's departure the Russians hosted their British guests in a banquet. During the event Commander Geoffrey Sladen confided to his Soviet counterpart that his wife had trouble pushing her pram through the snow. Immediately, the Russian admiral knew the solution. His wife needed a reindeer to help her!

The next morning, as the British crew prepared their departure, a large bag containing a young deer and a barrel of moss duly appeared on the dockside. Not wishing to disappoint their hosts, it was decided to take her on board. The animal was lowered through the torpedo tube of the submarine as it was thought that it would sleep in the torpedo and food store. She received the nickname Pollyanna after the base.

Conditions soon proved difficult, however. The Russians had believed that the submarine would return immediately to the UK. Instead, it was sent on a six-week tour of duty. Unfortunately for the deer, the moss soon ran out but luckily she seemed to appreciate the scraps from the galley and the odd navigation chart. She also gorged herself on condensed milk. Instead of sleeping in the torpedo store as expected, Pollyanna preferred to settle down under the captain's bed. The burly commander, it seems, had become something of a mother figure. With fifty-six crewmen and a rather smelly deer the air on board became rather putrid. However, whenever the submarine surfaced it was the special guest, panting heavily, who managed to force her way up the hatchway first.

On arrival in Blyth in Northumberland a new problem was encountered. The reindeer had grown in size and could not be pulled out through the hatch. She had to be trussed up and pulled through with the help of a dockside winch and a broom.

Afterwards, Pollyanna was found a home in Regent's Park Zoo. She never forgot her experience and if she ever heard a siren she always lowered her head as if getting ready to run to the hatch. She died in February 1946. Ironically, this was only a few days after HMS *Trident* itself was decommissioned.

29. German U-Boats Have 'Happy Times'

During the 1930s Hitler had concentrated on building up a large surface fleet at the expense of his U-boat arm. Unfortunately for the German war effort, when war came in September 1939 these ships, although impressive in power and size, were far too few in number to affect the course of the war. With the defeat of France in June 1940, however, it soon became abundantly clear that the small U-boat fleet was now to be an important weapon in Hitler's war against Britain. The hope was that the British could be starved into submission by cutting their imports upon which they depended.

The 'Battle of the Atlantic' was to be key to Britain's survival. In 1938 the British relied on imports of 68 million tons of dry cargo, but the U-boats were to cause this to be more than halved by 1942. In 1940 the Commander of the U-boat fleet, Admiral Karl Doenitz, reckoned he could bring Britain to her knees if he had 300 submarines; in fact at that time he only had twenty serviceable ones. However, Hitler now gave the go-ahead for a massive expansion.

By 1941 U-boats were hunting across the Atlantic in large groups or 'wolf-packs'. Their prey were merchant ships carrying vital supplies from America for Britain's war-weary population. The U-boats lay in line waiting for the convoys with their naval escorts. The first half of 1941 was indeed a 'happy time'; for example, between April and June 1941 1,100,000 tons of Allied shipping was lost. Furthermore, in September 1941 the German B-Dienst naval intelligence service had broken British naval codes. It was a grim time.

The Germans did not have it all their own way, however. Bletchley Park, the British codebreaking facility, was able to break the German U-boat code called naval enigma in June 1941. This meant that many convoys were able to be rerouted, which resulted in a substantial diminution of shipping losses. Nevertheless, by the end of 1941 these losses were outstripping replacements by 7 million tons. It was still a dangerous situation.

The year 1942 did not see an easing of the situation for the Allies. In December 1941 Hitler had declared war on the USA. German U-boats were now free to sink a large number of unescorted American merchant ships on the US east coast. To add to the Allied problems the Germans had altered the machine that sent out the naval enigma code, and for most of 1942 Bletchley Park remained blind. In addition, Doenitz now had his 300 U-boats, and the impact was devastating. A second 'happy time' resulted in 4 million tons of shipping being lost in the first eight months of that year.

Churchill later declared 'the only thing that really frightened me during the war was the U-boat peril'. New strategies and new technology would be required if the Allies were to win the war.

30. The Merchant Navy Was the Forgotten Branch of Britain's Armed Services

The merchant navy represented the lifeblood of Britain during the war and kept her supplied with vital food and supplies. However, the immense sacrifice of the merchant navy has often been overlooked. Almost on a daily basis merchant seamen had to face the gauntlet of enemy submarines, capital ships and mines. As testament to this, during the course of the war Britain lost 2,426 merchant ships and 11,331,933 tons of shipping. The sad tally of merchant seamen lost was 29,180, which is a higher casualty figure proportionately than that suffered by the three other UK armed services.

Conditions were invariably treacherous, but perhaps the worst conditions were those encountered on the Arctic convoys that travelled around the North Cape of Norway to Archangel or Murmansk in the Soviet Union. Falling into the icy waters there could result in death in just a few minutes. But, of course, most merchant convoys were in the Atlantic.

Inevitably, there are various epic tales. One famous event was the case of the *San Demetrio*. She was sailing in convoy HX-84 in October 1940 crossing the Atlantic from Halifax, Nova Scotia to the UK. The convoy was attacked by the German heavy cruiser *Admiral Scheer*. The German ship soon sent several shells into the *San Demetrio*. As she was carrying aviation fuel it was decided to abandon ship and to make for the two lifeboats. One lifeboat, which included the captain, was picked up the next day. The other lifeboat containing sixteen men drifted for twenty-four hours. Incredibly, they then sighted their old abandoned ship still afloat and after some hesitation decided to reboard it. Lacking navigational equipment but somehow steering by using the sun, they managed to reach the UK after seven days. It was remarkable that only 200 of the 12,000 tons of aviation fuel were lost; even more so was the fact that as the crew had achieved their feat unassisted, they were entitled to £14,000 of salvage money, which they shared out among themselves.

Another example of remarkable survival is that of the freighter *Anglo-Saxon*. She set sail in August 1940 with a cargo of coal for Argentina as normal trade still took place during the war. Two hundred miles north of the Tropic of Cancer she was shelled by a German raider. Seven men made it to the small jolly boat. The boat drifted west for seventy days before two survivors staggered out onto a beach in the Bahamas. Unfortunately, one survivor later died on the journey home when his ship was sunk one day before it was due to reach England. Only one man, Robert Tapscott, eventually made it back to the UK.

It is no wonder then that over 600 decorations were awarded for gallantry. Every day those manning the merchant ships knew their lives were on the line. Sadly, the only recognition of their terrible losses is a single memorial on London's Tower Hill.

31. Hitler Was a Super Junkie

As the absolute dictator of the German Reich, Hitler was aware that he needed to be on top form, especially for all public appearances. He felt he could not be seen to be suffering from any ailments that might impinge on his performance and could be seen as weakness.

It was not just common colds that the Führer was concerned about. He also suffered from debilitating stomach cramps that would leave him doubled up in pain. In 1936 a quack doctor by the name of Theodor Morell came to his rescue by offering him regular injections of glucose and vitamins, and these successfully removed all symptoms.

By August 1941, however, with the war in Russia reaching a crucial phase, Hitler found himself in need of something stronger. Morell started to inject Hitler with a special concoction of his own, which included the sexual hormone Testoviron, Orchikrin (a derivative of bull's testicles) and extracts from other farm animals. Over time Morell used some eighty different medicinal cocktails.

The threat of impending defeat imposed further pressure on the all-powerful leader, who by 1943 required a still more powerful stimulant. Morell prescribed Eukodal, a derivative of opium, which bucked up the Führer no end. Hitler soon became addicted and the constant daily intake of these drugs (including cocaine) began to have a devastating impact on his body.

In the final stages of the war Hitler had visibly degenerated due to the drugs. His hands shook uncontrollably. His teeth were falling out and his organs were failing. The super druggie's body had reached a point of no return.

32. Pearl Harbour Wakes the Sleeping Giant

For some time during the 1930s Japan had become increasingly aggressive. In 1937 she had launched a war with China, which had featured numerous atrocities. Those with influence around the Japanese emperor declared, however, that if Japan was to become a truly great power it needed to acquire its own resources. Japan lacked raw materials and above all oil. Much of these resources had to be imported from America. The problem was that President Franklin D. Roosevelt was aiding China and imposing sanctions on the Japanese.

The military government in Tokyo came up with a plan. In a lightening campaign they would seize British, French and Dutch colonies in south-east Asia along with the American-controlled Philippines in order to get hold of the resources they so desperately needed. In tandem with this they would strike at the US Pacific Fleet anchored in the island base of Pearl Harbour. It was estimated that the Japanese fleet could deal such a blow that America would need six months to rebuild its forces. This would be enough time for Japan to consolidate its new empire, also called the 'Greater East Asia Co-Prosperity Sphere'. With the Soviet Union no longer posing a threat, the end of 1941 seemed a good time to act.

The attack on Pearl Harbour was masterminded by the Commander-in-Chief of the Japanese Navy, Admiral Isoruku Yamamoto. His massive strike force set sail for Pearl Harbour on 26 November. It contained six aircraft carriers with 423 warplanes in total. They were flanked by an armada of heavy cruisers, battleships and destroyers. Having maintained radio silence the Americans were unaware of the fleets arrival north-east of the Hawaiian Islands on 6 December. No declaration of war had been received in Washington and surprise was complete when early the next morning the various bombers, torpedo planes and zero fighters went in for the kill. The radio signal went out 'Tora! Tora! Tora!'

With the American ships moored closely together, they made easy targets. Two waves of attack went in and the damage wreaked was immense. Two battleships, the *Arizona* and *Oklahoma*, were completely destroyed – the latter capsized trapping 429 men. Three other large ships, the *California, West Virginia* and *Nevada*, were sunk and many other vessels were damaged. Over 300 American planes had been destroyed or badly damaged on the ground. The Japanese pilots were jubilant and believed they had scored a great victory.

Appearances, however, were deceptive. Victory in the Pacific War would depend on eliminating the opponent's aircraft carriers. By sheer chance all six American carriers, which were normally moored in Pearl Harbour, had been absent at the time. In addition, all the ships apart from *Arizona* and *Oklahoma* were soon repaired. America would, within a few months, be able to exact her revenge.

The next day President Roosevelt described 7 December 1941 as 'a day that will live in infamy'. It had been an unprovoked attack that now roused an industrial giant out of its isolationist slumber.

33. Britain and America Begin Their Collaboration

The Anglo-American partnership is one of the most remarkable stories of the war. The closeness of the collaboration was unique and it was certainly not reproduced to the same degree with the other ally, Soviet Russia. Although there were often trials and tribulations, the two sides worked closely together on strategy and in the sharing of information.

Since the outbreak of war in Europe President Roosevelt had endeavoured to give his support to an embattled Britain while seemingly maintaining an isolationist stance at home. By the autumn of 1940 substantial British orders of planes and tanks had been placed, and in the Destroyers for Bases Agreement America supplied fifty surplus warships to Britain in exchange for eight British overseas bases. However, it was only after Roosevelt's re-election in November 1940 that the collaboration deepened. However, the president had promised to keep America out of the war so he had to tread a careful path. Nevertheless, by the Lend-Lease arrangement of March 1941 America agreed to supply vast quantities of armaments and food to Britain on credit. Collaboration was further extended by America stepping up its support to Britain in the Battle of the Atlantic.

Even though America was not at war Roosevelt agreed to meet Churchill at Placentia Bay off the Newfoundland coast in August 1941. Churchill arrived in grand style aboard the massive 35,000 ton battleship HMS *Prince of Wales* while Roosevelt was on board the cruiser USS *Augusta*. The two leaders immediately established an excellent rapport and agreed what would happen should America join in the war. Roosevelt proudly unfurled his 'Atlantic Charter', which would set out the guiding principles of the Allied side. These included the right of self-determination of all nations, the right of peoples to choose their own governments and 'freedom from fear and want'.

After Pearl Harbour America had clearly entered the war, but only against Japan. Fortunately, Hitler himself soon declared war on America, thereby allowing Roosevelt to keep his promise of not deliberately involving America in the war. Churchill arrived in Washington at the end of December and it was immediately agreed to keep to the strategy already decided earlier in the year. It was to be Europe first. The war against Japan would be a secondary front. Churchill also won over the president to the idea that there should be no costly early attempts at a cross-Channel invasion of France in 1942 as favoured by some American generals. The Allies should focus instead on defeating the Axis in the desert and Italy. This was to be Churchill's famous 'Mediterranean strategy'. Roosevelt, it seemed, was happy to follow the experienced British premier's views.

The result was that on 8 November 1942 the Allies launched the Anglo-American invasion of French North Africa, codenamed 'Operation Torch'. The Americans had arrived in the European theatre and for the moment were at Churchill's bidding.

34. The Japanese Take South-East Asia by Storm

You may recall that Pearl Harbour was part of a two-pronged master plan (*see* Fact 32). While America was reeling from the assault on its navy, Japanese imperial forces would overrun Dutch, French, British and American possessions in South East Asia. Within six months the Japanese were able to seize control of one-sixth of the earth's surface. The story is one that is reminiscent of the German invasion of the Soviet Union in June 1941. Whereas Stalin failed to interpret Hitler's thought processes, Britain and America, likewise, seriously miscalculated the enemy's capabilities and intentions.

On 8 December the simultaneous assaults began. To begin with Wake Island, Guam and Hong Kong were seized. There was a small Commonwealth army of Australian, Canadian, Indian and British forces in Hong Kong but these were soon forced back and nearly 11,000 surrendered on Christmas Day. At the same time Japanese forces swept through neutral Thailand and set about the invasion of Burma. Meanwhile the Japanese 25th Army landed in Malaya intent on seizing British-controlled Singapore. The American colony of the Philippines also came under attack.

The Americans put up epic resistance but were taken by surprise and overwhelmed by sheer numbers. General Douglas MacArthur had 24,000 men and a scratch force of Filipinos to defend the islands. Unfortunately, a large part of his air force was destroyed on the ground from the start, leaving his forces vulnerable to attack. By 23 December he had abandoned Manila, the capital, and had retreated into the jungles and swamps of the Bataan Peninsula and the island of Corregidor. Surrounded and facing a Japanese army of 200,000 men, MacArthur was ordered to leave the Philippines by President Roosevelt. He famously promised 'I shall return'. The Japanese captured 78,000 American and Filipino soldiers and cruelly sent them on the infamous 65-mile 'Bataan Death March'. On Corregidor 2,000 US cavalry troops held out in caves until 6 May.

In Singapore the story was less heroic. The island of Singapore on the end of the Malaysian Peninsula was considered by many in Britain to be an impregnable fortress. The British commander there was General A. E. Percival. With protruding front teeth, he cut a rather unprepossessing figure who was all too easily blamed for the debacle that followed. In reality he had been dealt a poor hand by the government in London. Most of the troops at his disposal to take on the Japanese were untrained Indians and Australians. He had no tanks and had woefully insufficient air and naval support. No wonder then that when the Japanese launched their offensive against the north of Malaya on 7 December 1941, they were able to move swiftly down the peninsula, often making use of bicycles, and easily outflanking British imperial forces, which were soon forced back onto the island. The myth of Singapore's impregnability was soon revealed. Makeshift defences were soon overwhelmed and Percival surrendered after only two weeks, and nearly 139,000 men were marched into captivity. The Japanese had fewer men but had lost only 9,824 soldiers. For Churchill it was 'The worst disaster and largest capitulation in British history'.

Overnight the apparently invincible Japanese had amassed a huge empire.

35. A LEG IS PARACHUTED IN FOR A BRITISH ACE PILOT

Wing Commander Douglas Bader is one of the more extraordinary characters of the Second World War. Having lost both legs prior to the outbreak of war in 1939, he was nevertheless determined to play his full part in the conflict. He proved to be an ace pilot and a thorn in the side of the enemy in more ways than one.

As a young man he cut a dashing and rather impetuous figure. He loved to show off his piloting skills and took his daredevil aerobatics to the limit. In late 1931 his luck ran out when a wing tip touched the ground and his plane crashed. He laconically wrote 'Bad show' in the log book. Leg amputations followed and his career seemed over as he was invalided out. However, when war broke out the rule book was waived and he was soon able to show his prowess. He served valiantly in the Battle of Britain and was credited with twenty aerial victories. By 1941 he had risen to the position of Wing Commander.

During 1941 Bader undertook several sweeps over occupied France. Then one day in August disaster struck. While hunting down some German ME 109 fighters that he espied some way below him, he suddenly realised that he had been hit. It was a mad scramble to bail out made especially difficult as he had to extricate his artificial legs, one of which he had to leave in the cockpit.

He was captured by the Germans and taken to St Omer 20 miles from the French coast. His captors were sympathetic to his plight. He befriended Adolf Galland, himself an air ace of the Third Reich, who contacted the British authorities. With the express permission of Reich Marshall Hermann Goering the Germans had a singular request. They wanted a prosthetic leg for a captured pilot. One British plane would be allowed through in order to carry out the special mission. In due course, a Blenheim bomber arrived and dropped a canister by parachute. Inside was the leg together with some tobacco, chocolate and other assorted wartime treats placed there by his wife, Thelma.

The Germans soon learned to regret their kindness. In no time he set about trying to escape from the very same hospital where he was recovering. The attempt failed but he was involved in numerous other unsuccessful escape plans. The Germans became exasperated and even threatened to confiscate his legs. Finally, he was moved to the impregnable Colditz Castle, which the Germans used for serial escape artists. He remained there until April 1945.

On his arrival back home he was feted as a hero and as one of the 'few' in the Battle of Britain. After the war he was promoted to Group Captain but later he preferred to work for Dutch Shell Oil as an executive. In 1956 a film was made about his life entitled, *Reach for the sky*. It featured Kenneth Moore as Bader and received the BAFTA Award for 'Best British Film'.

36. Leningrad Was Besieged for 900 Days

Hitler's Operation Barbarossa had initially resulted in devastating losses of men and territory for the Soviet Union (Fact 26). Prior to the war Leningrad, today's St Petersburg, was the second city of the Soviet Union with a population of 3,500,000. The swift advance of the German armies, together with Finnish forces from the north, meant that already by the second week of September 1941 the city was surrounded with much of the population sealed up inside. Rather than launching a direct assault Hitler decided to starve the city out. Leningrad would then be razed to the ground.

Every effort had been made to stave off the Nazi advance. Citizens' militia had been rushed out to desperately dig defensive lines but these had failed to hold the enemy. Stalin brought in General Zhukov to take control of the city's defences. Zhukov ordered that the guns be wrested from the ships of the Baltic fleet and instead be placed on trains or dug into fortified positions. Defensive perimeters were established and fierce discipline was imposed. Any slackers or deserters faced summary execution. The constant shelling and bombing by the enemy made life grim and soon electricity and phone lines were cut.

As many as 490,000 men, women and children had been evacuated before the siege, but this still left a vast population to feed. Ration cards were issued but the food available was already meagre. By November the situation was critical with only 8 ounces of adulterated bread available per day for workers and soldiers; the rest got half this. This was patently insufficient for human survival. At first people resorted to eating their pets. Some imaginative people made soup from glue and leather. As the situation deteriorated perhaps thousands turned to cannibalism. By January between 5,000 and 6,000 people were dying every day from famine with many others losing their lives due to enemy action.

The situation was not entirely hopeless, however. Leningrad still had access to Lake Ladoga, which lay in the vicinity. When the mighty Russian winter set in the great lake froze over to such a depth that it was possible to drive vehicles across it. It was soon dubbed the 'Road of Life' and some food and other supplies were able to be brought in. By January the bread ration was slightly increased. In addition, more than 500,000 emaciated Leningraders were evacuated via this route. But the ice road was not without its risks. German bombing or a slight thaw could mean a lorry suddenly sinking without trace into the murky depths.

Despite the harrowing conditions the people of Leningrad refused to surrender and the city somehow survived that first terrible winter. But the cost had been enormous. By the end of the siege, which was lifted in January 1944 (actually 872 days), perhaps 1.5 million Soviet citizens had lost their lives there. It was one of the longest and most destructive sieges in history.

Hitler had hubristically expected Leningrad to 'fall like a leaf'. The stoical Russian people defied the Führer.

37. The Wannsee Conference Starts the Holocaust in Earnest

Adolf Hitler, in a speech in 1939, had declared that if war broke out then it would lead to the destruction of the Jewish race in Europe. What this exactly meant was unclear. Prior to the war Jews in Germany had found themselves excluded from society and many had been encouraged to leave. After the occupation of Poland in August 1939, Jews there had been forced to live in ghettos. Life there was extremely harrowing, but there was no clear plan for mass extermination of these poor souls. Hitler even discussed the possibility of resettlement of the Jewish population in Madagascar. Indeed after the invasion of the Soviet Union in June 1941 another plan had been to round up all Jewish people there and march them to the other side of the Ural Mountains and into Siberia. However, with the war in Russia entering something of a stalemate this would no longer be possible. In any case by the autumn of 1941 Hitler had already decided that he wanted a 'Final Solution' to the Jewish problem, which meant the extermination of all Jews across Europe.

Reinhard Heydrich had risen rapidly through the ranks of the SS (Hitler's black-uniformed agents of terror). By 1941 he was second only to Heinrich Himmler, the leader of the whole wretched apparatus. Heydrich had the nicknames the 'Blond Beast' and the 'Hangman' for good reason. Since the invasion of the Soviet Union he had been responsible for setting up squads of 'Special Action Groups' (or *Einsatzgruppen*) whose sole task was the liquidation of Jews and communist party members. However, the mass shooting of these people was an inefficient and unpleasant process; even Himmler found the whole thing distasteful. Heydrich was given the task of organising a speedier way to deal with the millions of Jews being rounded up.

For some time during 1941 experiments had been taking place in concentration camps in order to facilitate the process. Heydrich had pioneered the use of mobile gas vans and these were used to kill Jews in Chelmno in Poland in the autumn of 1941. In addition Zyklon B, crystallised cyanide gas, was already being used in Auschwitz around this time. However, all these initiatives were uncoordinated and haphazard.

On 20 January 1942 Heydrich chaired a conference at Lake Wannsee just outside Berlin. Its purpose was to make the 'Final Solution' official policy and to coordinate the action across various ministries of government. Fifteen SS and government officials were present. What is chilling about the meeting is the matter-of-fact manner in which the genocide of Europe's Jewish population is discussed. The word 'kill' is never used in the final document; instead there were euphemisms such as 'Final Solution' and 'deportation to the east'. Afterwards the whole process of the Holocaust became systematised and accelerated.

Whether Hitler had always intended such a horrific and brutal policy is a moot point, but certainly the cloak of war made such an act possible.

38. THE BATTLE OF MIDWAY IS DECISIVE

After the attack on Pearl Harbour (Fact 32) the Japanese advance across South Asia had seemed relentless. Australia and India were clearly under threat. However, the American Pacific fleet had not been dealt the knockout blow the Japanese had hoped for. Indeed, as the Japanese themselves had feared, within six months the Americans were able to assemble a sizeable naval force capable of taking on their rampant foe.

By the beginning of May 1942 enemy forces were getting worryingly near to Australia. A Japanese naval force was closing in on Papua New Guinea with the intention of staging a seaborne capture of the main town, Port Moresby. The American Task Force 17 was despatched to intercept the Japanese fleet. It soon became known as the Battle of the Coral Sea and was to be the first sea battle in history in which neither side saw or engaged each other directly. Both opponents launched fighter planes from their respective aircraft carriers with the intention of knocking out the other's carrier force. In a topsy-turvy conflict there were only a few serious hits, causing the sinking of one Japanese light carrier and the damaging of two of their heavy carriers. As a result the Japanese decided to abandon their planned invasion. The Americans had only lost one carrier. Their opponents, however, were convinced that another carrier, *Yorktown*, had also been sunk. Although severely damaged, in a remarkable effort American repair teams refitted her and got her back into service within forty-eight hours. This was soon to prove crucial.

The commander of the Japanese Combined Fleet, Admiral Yamamoto, believed that with the loss of the *Yorktown* the Americans would lack air power. He could now afford to take control of Midway Island (within striking distance of Pearl Harbour) and at the same time lure the American fleet into a trap. Japanese intelligence was poor, however, and Yamamoto was unaware that the Americans had broken their codes and were waiting for them. The Japanese attack force contained a massive armada of 165 warships including several carriers. Initially, they put their main effort into attacking Midway unaware of the American presence. Admiral Nagumo, who commanded four carriers, at first kept ninety-three reserve planes fitted with torpedoes ready should the American fleet be sighted. He now made a fatal error. As no Americans were reported he countermanded that even these planes should now to be fitted with incendiary and fragmentation bombs for the attack on Midway. This changeover would take an hour. As luck would have it fifteen minutes later American reconnaissance planes were suddenly sighted. Nagumo pondered what to do and eventually decided to refit the torpedoes. Matters were further confused when returning fighters were allowed to land on the carriers. Disaster soon followed. With the planes sitting prone on the decks surrounded by fuel and explosive ordnance the carriers were dangerously exposed. Waves of American dive bombers swooped in and by the end of the day all four carriers had been sunk.

It was a decisive blow from which Japan never recovered.

39. The Jerry Can Proved a Winner

The Desert War swung to and fro across North Africa for three years between 1940 and 1943. The arrival of German forces in March 1941 shifted the balance back in favour of Axis forces and by 1942 British forces had retreated back into Egypt. However, it was not all bad news. Whenever the Afrika Korps was forced into a withdrawal, British 'Tommies' were always pleased to pick up the 'Jerry' (German) cans left behind.

So what was so special about this fuel can? For British tank crews it was clearly a superior design to the 4-gallon can they had to use. For one thing the German can was robust: it was made of pressed steel with cross-like indentations on the sides for extra strength. Compared with any previous designs it was also user-friendly. At the top of the can there was an arrangement of three parallel handles. This was extremely practical as it allowed for two people to carry the can at the same time and it could be easily passed to another person. In addition, the top had a secure cam lever release mechanism, which was also leakproof and allowed for smooth pouring.

The British 4-gallon cans, on the other hand, were known as 'flimsies' as they were liable to develop punctures and leak, especially when driven over rough desert terrain. After one journey they often had to be disposed of.

The Jerry can design, however, is still used in many armies to this day. Clearly a winner!

40. PQ17 Was the Convoy from Hell

As mentioned before the British ran convoys across the North Sea to Russian Arctic ports via the North Cape of Norway (Fact 30). These convoys were particularly vulnerable to attack in summertime. This was because along the Norwegian coast the Germans had a vast array of planes, U-boats and capital ships (including the fearsome battleship *Tirpitz*) whose sole intention was to annihilate these very convoys.

One unfortunate convoy was PQ 17, which set sail from Iceland on 27 June 1942. It contained thirty-six merchant ships and a large close escort of six destroyers and fifteen other vessels. In addition, another large force under Admiral John Tovey containing two battleships and various cruisers would provide protection but only as far as Bear Island near the North Cape. It was feared these important vessels would be too vulnerable beyond this point. From 2 July the enemy attacks started and Admiral Tovey soon withdrew. The close escort continued to offer support but this too was withdrawn when the admiralty received news that the *Tirpitz* had left the Altenfiord where it was lurking.

Immediately the disastrous order was given to 'scatter' the convoy. Ironically, unknown to the British the *Tirpitz* had soon returned to port. Alas for the convoy it was now completely at the mercy of German dive-bombers and U-boats. By the time the convoy reached port in Russia only eleven ships had survived. Lost at sea were 430 tanks, 210 aircraft and 3,350 other vehicles. It had been a calamity.

41. THE AMERICANS HAVE A 'GOOD WAR'

America's experience of the war was certainly different from many other combatant nations. For many peoples the war brought massive destruction, economic devastation and huge losses of soldiers and civilians. In addition, many suffered the hardship and suffering of enemy occupation. Not only did the USA avoid all of these, she even emerged from the war as a world superpower.

Ironically, the war brought relief from suffering for many in America. The Great Depression of the 1930s had brought harrowing times in the form of massive unemployment. Despite the frantic efforts of President Roosevelt to ease the situation, by 1940 the unemployment level still remained at around 8 million. However, once the American economy was completely mobilised for the war effort, full employment soon followed.

Economic production actually doubled during the war and the size of the economy grew likewise. This had an impact for ordinary Americans who saw their personal incomes rise by as much as 200 per cent. Although the government imposed controls on prices and wages there was little rationing and the lights never went out. Civilian consumption rose by more than 20 per cent. It is no wonder that many Americans welcomed the war. They had never had it so good.

There was also a general increase in social mobility. Many women were drafted into the munitions industry and into other 'men only' occupations – by 1944 they represented 36 per cent of the workforce. Large numbers of agricultural workers as well as African-Americans moved to the cities. Many young men who left their home districts for the first time saw new horizons either in the big cities or in the army.

Of course the war was not kind to everybody. For African-Americans the picture was rather mixed. Whereas they won the right to equality of treatment in the workplace, there were still severe racial tensions. For example, in 1943 a race riot in Detroit saw 100,000 people on the streets, which left thirty-four dead. In the army, segregation meant separate units for blacks and whites. However, many commentators see the war years as a positive turning point in the civil rights movement.

For the Japanese-Americans the war was, to put it mildly, rather unpleasant. After the attack on Pearl Harbour President Roosevelt issued Executive Order 9066, which resulted in the internment of 120,000 Japanese-Americans (two-thirds of whom were born in America) living on the west coast. They were given notice of a mere seventy-two hours before they were moved to isolated camps, where they lived in barrack-like cabins surrounded by barbed wire. It was not until two years later that they were finally allowed back home.

For those military personnel who died in the war (around 405,000) it was clearly not a good outcome, but even this figure represented a tiny fraction of the population. For the vast majority of Americans the war had clearly been beneficial.

42. Lend-Lease Was an American Lifeline That Helped All the Allies

One of the most amazing facts of the war is that America managed to fight a war on two fronts (Europe and the Pacific) and at the same time keep her allies supplied with immense quantities of tanks, vehicles and all manner of other wartime requisites. These deliveries represented a salvation for Britain and the Soviet Union who were the two main beneficiaries. (In total thirty-eight countries received help.) Not only did it permit these countries to survive, but it also enabled them to decisively turn the tide against their fearsome enemies.

When President Roosevelt proclaimed in December 1940 that America would become the 'arsenal of democracy', he was clearly signalling that his country would come to the aid of those countries fighting fascism. By the beginning of 1941 Roosevelt was becoming increasingly concerned about Britain's ability to prosecute the war. His proposal was to let Britain have the resources she needed for her defence without expecting any immediate payment. The problem was that America was not in the war and there was strong opposition from isolationists to the very notion of getting involved. Nevertheless, on 11 March 1941 the Lend-Lease Act was passed by congress. Roosevelt, rather disingenuously, compared it to a situation where you were merely lending your neighbour a hose when his house was on fire. Afterwards, it would be returned when the fire had been put out. However, nobody was seriously expecting Britain to return any battered or burnt-out tanks!

All American goods destined for Britain had to be transported across the Atlantic Ocean through the gauntlet of German U-boats. The British remained under strict rationing at this time, so to begin with the priority was food rather than tanks and planes, although these too were supplied. The first deliveries contained dried eggs, evaporated milk and spam. America provided enormous quantities of war material and in the end Britain and her empire had the lion's share, receiving $31 billion of the $50 billion spent under the scheme. It was an important lifeline.

For the Soviet Union, too, American help proved vital. Supplies arrived via Vladivostok, the Persian Gulf or the British Arctic convoys. Although the USSR produced prodigious quantities of planes and tanks herself, she was seriously lacking in many basics including food. The statistics are remarkable; for example, America provided the Soviets with more than half a million vehicles (including 200,000 Studebaker trucks on which the Russians placed their frightening Katyusha rockets), 380,000 field telephones, 956,000 miles of telephone wire and nearly 15 million pairs of boots. The omnipresent spam also found its way there in large quantities. And all this to a communist regime to which most Americans were bitterly opposed!

After the war Stalin publically played down the importance of Lend-Lease. Privately, however, he admitted that the Soviet Union could not have won the war without it. In the end Russia did repay her debt in 1990 while Britain was only able to pay hers off in 2006.

43. In Britain Everybody Is Mobilised for the War Effort

The approaching defeat of France in June 1940 meant that Britain would soon be alone in Europe. It was imperative that Britain should husband all her resources to the utmost. Her very survival depended on it. Not only was the U-boat war in the Atlantic threatening vital supplies, but she would need to summon all her manpower to increase armaments production, meet the needs of her armed forces and at the same time ensure farming continued its food output.

Britain's transformation to total war was indeed remarkable. The entire population was mobilised, meaning as many as 4.5 million men were placed under arms. Women, too, were conscripted and 500,000 were put into uniform. For the war effort a total of 16 million men and 7 million women were mobilised, giving a total of 22 million. The remaining 10 million people were housewives, children, invalids and so forth.

In September 1939 the government had announced that it was taking all necessary powers to mobilise its citizens. However, during the 'Phoney War' the effort was rather half-hearted. But with the defeat on the Continent in 1940 all this changed. In May 1940 the Emergency Powers Act was passed, which gave unprecedented powers of control over British citizens and their property. All work was divided into essential and non-essential and where possible everybody was directed into the former. Identity cards were introduced for rationing and to tighten control over the public.

The National Service No. 2 Act of December 1941 brought in conscription for women. Some would be 'directed' to industry while others were 'conscripted' into the auxiliary services. Women were categorised as 'mobile' or 'immobile'. Mobile ones were single and could be moved around the country whereas immobile ones were married perhaps with children and had to work nearer to home. Some young women were conscripted to work in the Women's Land Army and were expected to wear a radical uniform of fawn corduroy breeches or khaki-coloured dungarees, green jerseys and strong brogues or gumboots. In total by July 1943 there were 87,000 women working in this capacity. Sometimes the conditions were grim and the work could be tough with long hours on isolated farms. These women had to deal with any task given them, including muck spreading and rat-catching!

The real threat of invasion in 1940 also led to the creation of the Home Guard. This was composed of those too old or too young to serve in the regular armed forces. Poor planning meant that initially for the 1.5 million volunteers there was a distinct lack of weaponry. Many were reduced to wielding pikes and truncheons. And it is true that some elderly volunteers really had fought in the colonial war in the Sudan in 1898.

In the precarious position that Britain found herself in the early stages of the war it was absolutely vital that the population was mobilised as efficiently as possible. Churchill's government was awarded dictatorial powers over its citizens, but everybody knew it was necessary for survival.

44. The British Wartime Diet Was Not So Bad

Rationing was a necessity in Britain because of her position as an industrialised nation and as a net importer of goods; for example, 70 per cent of her cheese and sugar and 80 per cent of her fruit was imported. Not only was the government keen to reduce unnecessary expenditure, but there was a problem of actually importing foodstuffs across the U-boat-infested Atlantic.

The first rationed goods were butter, sugar and ham. Later on, from time to time, meats and cheese were restricted as well as margarine, cooking fats, eggs and milk. Bread was not rationed but to save waste more was extracted from the wheat and it had a different colour and texture. This was termed the 'National Loaf' and in essence was the first wholewheat bread. It turned out to be very unpopular. At the end of the war people demanded their white bread back!

People were also encouraged to grow more food in back gardens, allotments and national parks.

Nevertheless, despite all the restrictions the diet of ordinary people did get better. The unhealthy pre-war diet was improved and supplemented by a better eating regime; for example, sugars and fats were reduced and vitamins were added to flour and margarine. Children got extra milk, fruit juice and cod liver oil. The health of young people improved and this was especially so for working-class children. In addition people ate more of their own fresh vegetables that they grew themselves. And then there was the National Loaf! There were certainly some positives.

45. Operation Blue Starts Off Well

After the bitter winter of 1941–42 and the German retreat before Moscow the front had stabilised. Hitler decided that the main offensive of 1942 would not be directed against Moscow as everybody, including his own generals, expected but towards the south. Operation Blue, as it was codenamed, would be divided into two parts: Army Group B would drive east and take Stalingrad to cover Army Group A, which would continue south-eastwards and capture the oil wells of Baku in the Caucasus. The aim was to deny the Soviet Union its resource base and to seize these for herself.

The offensive was launched on 28 June and from the beginning it went well. The morale of Soviet forces was already low due to the massive defeats in the previous year and in the spring. It is believed that the Soviet Union lost an estimated 1,400,000 men in the first six months of 1942 alone. German commanders were then easily able to achieve their initial objectives with more straightforward victories. Within a month the northern army group was within striking distance of Stalingrad while the southern group had crossed the River Don and was poised to move on the Caucasus.

These advances sent shock waves through the Soviet people and establishment. Discipline was breaking down in the Russian armies and men abandoned their equipment rather than face the 'invincible' Germans. Stalin tried to restore order by issuing his famous decree entitled 'Not a Step Back', which set out more severe punishments for cowardice in the field. Nevertheless, the Nazi advance continued unabated. As before, the reason for these endless defeats lay with Stalin himself, who remained intent on continuously launching reckless, ill-prepared counter-offensives against a superior enemy. These constant defeats could only provoke demoralisation.

In the south Army Group A made good headway across the open steppe and by the end of August had reached the Caucasus Mountains. However, they found their way barred through the passes by Soviet infantry units. A section of the army group drove eastwards towards the oil centres of Groznyi and Maikop, but eventually ground to a halt due to increasing Soviet resistance, supply problems and inclement weather. The German spearhead never reached the oil wells or the Caspian Sea. By the end of the year Hitler ordered the army group to pull back.

On 23 August units of Army Group B reached the Volga River. German forces were soon penetrating Stalingrad and it seemed that within a few days the city would fall. By 13 September General Paulus, commander of the German 6th Army, was preparing for a final push on the last remaining pockets of Soviet resistance. With heroic and unimaginable sacrifice the defenders held on. The city had refused to fall and fresh men and supplies were constantly ferried across the Volga in support. Both sides were now joined in a desperate and seemingly endless hand-to-hand struggle. However, Stalin was waiting to spring a trap.

For the Germans Operation Blue had started well but would end in disaster.

46. In the Ukraine Factories and Workers Are Transported Eastwards

One of the reasons that the Soviet Union was able to achieve a military turnaround by the end of 1942 was due to the incredible transportation of men and machines out of the Ukraine in the second half of 1941. It was often carried out under the most arduous of circumstances with German forces perhaps only hours away as complete factories, together with their workforces, were placed onto trains and moved wholesale to the Urals or Siberia. As many as 2,600 factories were transported in this way.

Even more incredible was the vast exodus of people who accompanied these factories or sought to escape the invader. It is believed as many as 25 million men, women and children left their homes. Many went on foot.

The journey there was not always the most difficult part. Very often the new factories were to be set up on undeveloped sites in the open countryside. Sometimes the conditions were seemingly impossible with permafrost and a lack of food and shelter. At one tank factory it was reported that 8,000 female workers were living in industrial bunkers – literally holes in the ground. Nevertheless, despite these wretched conditions Russian workers were soon able to reconstruct these factories to get them fully operational again.

The results were staggering. The Nazi onslaught had reduced the Soviet economy to a mere rump of its former self, but by the last half of 1942 it managed to turn out 13,000 tanks and 15,000 aircraft and even outstrip what Nazi Germany produced in a whole year.

47. The Burma Campaign Marked the Longest Retreat in British Military History

You may recall that at the end of 1941 the Japanese had launched offensives that had captured Hong Kong and would soon overrun Singapore. However, the Japanese had not waited for the fall of Singapore before extending their offensive campaign. Already at the end of January 1942 their forces had crossed over the Siam (Thailand) frontier and entered Burma.

Burma had become part of the British Empire when Churchill's father, Lord Randolph Churchill, had annexed it in 1886 while secretary for India. For the Japanese Burma was a vital military objective. Strategically it could be a launch pad for an invasion of India but more importantly it cut the Allies' Burma Road, which was a major land route into China. For some time the Americans had been providing much-needed supplies to the Chinese via this road and the Japanese were determined to sever the link. In addition, Burma was rich in oil and minerals.

As elsewhere the British military thinking was that because of the lack of good metalled roads and the thick jungle Burma was inaccessible for the enemy. They were about to be in for a shock. Only two divisions were available to stave off the attack – the British 1st Burma Division and the poorly trained 17th Indian Division (staffed by British officers). Despite the arrival of some reinforcements British forces would be woefully inadequate.

Rangoon, the capital, lay on the southern coast and was clearly vulnerable. Attempts to hold back the Japanese offensive soon proved fruitless, but British forces under the command of Sir Harold Alexander managed to extricate themselves just in time. These troops now had to endure a long march into the interior of Burma relentlessly pursued by a rampant Japanese foe. Their eventual destination would be India.

The first town on the way was Mandalay. British and Commonwealth soldiers had to struggle through the jungle at the hottest time of the year. The Japanese were now not the only enemy they had to contend with as the jungle was alive with nasties such as 15-inch poisonous centipedes, spiders the size of plates, and leeches. In addition, soldiers soon picked up diseases such as malaria, dysentery, typhus and jungle sores. Above all there was a scarcity of water and the troops often became numb with exhaustion.

Alexander and Major-General Bill Slim managed to skilfully keep the troops just ahead of the enemy despite the attempts of the Japanese to use the rivers to outflank them. Mandalay was reached safely but soon had to be abandoned in April for fear of encirclement. Eventually, after another month of forced marches a rather bedraggled and rag-tag army staggered into Assam in India.

The Burmese Army had marched an incredible 1,000 miles, which ranks as the longest retreat in British military history. Despite being constantly harried and without regular supplies, they had somehow avoided collapse and rout. Excellent generalship from Alexander and Slim had saved the empire and India from disaster.

48. Shostakovich Shows Solidarity with the Besieged Leningraders

Dmitri Shostakovich is remembered as one of the great composers of Communist Russia. When German forces reached the outskirts of Leningrad in September 1941 he found himself, like so many ordinary Russians, unable to escape. There was no alternative but to stay and suffer the siege.

Shostakovich had already started on his Seventh Symphony before the war began but continued to work hard at it even as bombs and shells exploded around him. Those who heard his first two movements were enthralled. After a month he was evacuated out of Leningrad and the composer set about quickly finishing his masterpiece. The first performance was aired in March 1942 on Soviet radio. The first movement especially struck a chord with its famous 'invasion theme'. The score was soon flown out to London and America where performances received critical acclaim.

Leningraders, however, had to wait longer to hear the symphony. The Leningrad Radio Orchestra had trouble collecting together their players due to the dreadful rigours of the siege. Eventually, after much practice and after receiving extra rations, the symphony was duly played on 9 August. It was a momentous occasion. Prior to the concert Soviet forces fired a massive salvo of shells onto the besieging Germans to ensure their silence. Then the masterpiece was played. Loudspeakers even relayed it to enemy. The music unleashed a massive outpouring of emotion as it seemed to encapsulate all the horrific suffering of the people there.

49. Bletchley Was the Golden Goose That Never Cackled

During much of the war the Allies held an important advantage over the Axis enemy. The secret codes that were transmitted by their armed forces were picked up and eventually broken by Britain's codebreaking establishment in Bletchley Park, near Milton Keynes. The enigma machine used by German armed forces to send their encoded messages seemed impregnable as the odds of breaking it were 159 million million million to one. How it was achieved is a remarkable story.

The British were lucky in their enterprise from the start as Polish codebreakers managed to smuggle two examples of the machine out of Warsaw just before Nazi forces arrived. With help from the Poles the British experts could see how it operated and could begin to crack it. However, it was a daunting task. The machine looked something like a typewriter with three to five rotor wheels in the top part and a plug board in the lower section. The complexity of the machine meant that there were over 17,000 different settings. Once a letter was pressed an electrical impulse was sent twice through the system and eventually a different letter would emerge on a display panel. The messages themselves were sent using radio waves, which would then be picked up and sent on to Bletchley. What was received looked like gobbledegook.

To begin with the codebreaking was agonisingly slow. Mathematicians, crossword solvers and top chess players were set to work with their crib sheets, but they could take days or weeks to crack a single message, by which time their information had become largely redundant. A further problem was that the settings were changed daily by the Germans according to a secret code book. Added to this each section of the German armed forces had a different system. Something needed to be done to speed up the whole process.

Alan Turing, a fellow of the University of Cambridge and something of a mathematical genius, had the answer. He introduced his 'bombes', which were fast-running electrical machines that could test possible settings at incredible speeds. Now the codes could often be cracked within hours.

Turing's contribution did not end there. By 1943 one frustrating code still eluded the Bletchley team. This was the one used by Hitler himself when communicating with his generals. His machine was called Lorenz and had as many as twelve rotor wheels, making it the most formidable of all. Turing had drawn up a plan for a computer prior to the war and the Bletchley people now used that model to create the first programmable electronic computer in order to crack Lorenz. This new machine, dubbed 'Colossus', could process characters at 5,000 characters per second. Soon Hitler's messages were laid before the Allied top brass in almost real time.

'Ultra', as the codebreakers' information was called, had a decisive impact in the war, especially in such conflicts as the U-boat war in the Atlantic, the desert war and D-Day. Churchill called Bletchley his 'golden goose that never cackled' as its secrets were never revealed to the enemy.

50. MONTY SENDS THE 'DESERT FOX' PACKING

By July 1942 Erwin Rommel, the commander of German forces in North Africa, had pushed British and Commonwealth forces 570 miles back across Libya and into Egypt. His army was now within striking distance of Alexandria and the Suez Canal. Their capture would be a serious blow to the British war effort in the Mediterranean, the Middle East and beyond.

Rommel had built up quite a reputation for himself due to his skilful and imaginative use of his panzer forces. British troops had called him the 'Desert Fox' while the British Eighth Army, which opposed him, was dubbed the 'Desert Rats'. For the moment the British had managed to avoid disaster by holding Rommel at a line called El Alamein. Churchill had expressed his strong displeasure with the performance of his commanders thus far in the desert war. So out went one lot of generals and in came Lieutenant-General Bernard Montgomery or 'Monty'.

Montgomery immediately set about restoring morale. He exuded self-confidence and decisiveness and told the troops that there could be no further withdrawals. Rommel could and would be defeated. The new British commander had a couple of aces up his sleeve, however. For one thing he knew that Rommel's Axis forces were seriously overstretched due to the 2,000-mile supply line from Tunisia. From the codebreakers at Bletchley Park (FACT 49) he knew exactly Rommel's situation and his plans. In addition, British forces were now being plentifully resupplied with tanks, artillery and men. By the autumn Montgomery had an advantage of two to one in military forces at his disposal. This meant that when the next battle came Rommel would almost inevitably be on the back foot.

Montgomery planned the battle meticulously. When it came on 23 October it was not a battle of manoeuvre.

The Germans were at first bludgeoned with a massive artillery barrage before infantry and armour were pushed forward with the intention of punching a hole in the German lines. However, Axis forces were well dug in behind miles of minefields. It was not until 3 November, ten days later, that Rommel's German and Italian forces fled the battlefield. Hitler had commanded him to stay and fight to the last man – 'Victory or death'. The German commander, however, wisely disobeyed this insane order and headed back westwards across the desert.

For the Allies it marked the first defeat of German armed forces in the west. It was also the last great British and Commonwealth victory in the war before the Americans joined in. Bells rang out across Britain to celebrate the victory. Churchill noted later that 'Before Alamein we never had a victory, after Alamein we never had a defeat.'

The victory was not total, however. Rommel had managed to extricate the remnants of his forces and escape back to Tunisia. Many felt that Monty had let the Germans off the hook. With only twenty tanks left surely Rommel's forces should have been wiped out there and then. As it was, the war there dragged on for another seven months.

51. Stalingrad Was a Huge Turning Point in the War

You may recall that the German offensive code-named Operation Blue had started well. Nazi forces had swept eastwards across the Ukraine, inflicted more massive defeats on the Soviets before reaching the Volga River. There was a feeling of euphoria in the German camp as it seemed that their Soviet enemy was finished. After such crushing defeats surely the enemy would be unable to muster any more armies.

Upon reaching Stalingrad, however, the resistance of the enemy suddenly stiffened. Despite continuing losses from the first day, Soviet forces refused to be bowed. During September and October the German 6th Army, aided by continual aerial bombardment, launched numerous offensives to take the city, but Soviet forces refused to crack.

Meanwhile, a new change of direction was happening in the Soviet army headquarters, or *Stavka*. Stalin by August 1942 had decided on a more collegiate approach to decision making. As the German forces entered Stalingrad the Soviet leader proposed the usual immediate counter-attack. When his two top generals, Zhukov and Vasilevsky, muttered something about 'another solution', Stalin famously turned round and asked 'what other solution?' For the first time Stalin was prepared to listen to his generals. Instead of attacking, his new team decided to let the Germans continue their advance into the city. New Soviet armies would be held in reserve, thoroughly trained and prepared until the propitious moment came for a mighty counter-punch.

Inside Stalingrad the battle became ever-more bitter, bringing unimaginable losses and suffering; for example, Rodimtsev's division of 10,000 men was reduced to only

320 in one short battle. The fighting was brutal with no quarter given. Strategic points such as the Red October Factory exchanged hands several times. Snipers were a continuous hazard. The Soviet hero was General Vasily Chuikov, who commanded the troops inside Stalingrad. His bunker was right in the front line and his ruthless and heroic leadership prevented the city from falling. However, one last final push by the Germans in November left the Soviets with just two small pockets supplied from across the Volga River. But still the city refused to fall.

Hitler, in a speech that month, had expressed his confidence that the battle would soon be over. However, at that very moment General Zhukov unleashed a vast double envelopment of Stalingrad. Romanian and Italian forces, guarding the flanks of the German Army to the north and south, were overwhelmed. The Soviet pincers linked up on 23 November leaving Von Paulus's forces trapped inside. General Manstein desperately tried to reach them with a relieving army, but it was of no avail. With few supplies getting in and with sub-zero temperatures, the end was inevitable. On the 2 February General Paulus formally surrendered his frostbitten and half-starved army.

Of an original German force of 275,000 men only 91,000 shuffled off into captivity. However, the Soviet losses in the Stalingrad campaign had amounted to over one million. For Hitler, though, it was a disaster and a turning point as for Nazi Germany these were irreparable losses.

52. Marshall Zhukov Was the Man Who Saved the Soviet Union

Marshall Georgi K. Zhukov was one of the most outstanding generals of the Second World War. He was a tough and decisive commander who time and time again won important battles when the future of his country hung in the balance. But perhaps his greatest contribution was his ability to stand up to the fearsome Soviet leader, Josef Stalin. It was Zhukov, and Zhukov alone, who had the courage to make the dictator see sense regarding his direction of the war. At Stalingrad, as we have seen (Fact 51), it proved crucial.

Zhukov started life as a humble shoemaker's son. During the First World War he was drafted into the imperial cavalry where he immediately showed promise and was awarded the Cross of St George twice for bravery. After the Russian Revolution in October 1917 he sided with the communists and fought for the Red Army. During the 1920s and 1930s he rapidly rose through the ranks and somehow survived the dictator's ferocious purges of the military top brass.

It would seem that Stalin liked or admired Zhukov, for in 1938 he was put in charge of a whole army group in the Russian Far East. Here he showed his abilities when a year later he inflicted a crucial defeat on the Japanese, who were pushing up through northern China. In January 1941 he was awarded the position of Chief of the General Staff but was dismissed after he disagreed with the Soviet leader over how to react to the Nazi invasion. Stalin despatched him off to command the reserve army outside Smolensk, where he inflicted the first setback on German forces. Perhaps as the result of this in September that year Stalin recalled him and sent him on missions to firstly save Leningrad and then later Moscow from the Nazis.

By 1942 he was rehabilitated and persuaded Stalin to accept his plans for the Battle of Stalingrad, which resulted in the first decisive victory. From then on he played an important role in Soviet triumphs all the way to the final battle for Berlin.

After the war Stalin became suspicious and jealous of this illustrious hero and gave him minor postings far from Moscow. After the death of Stalin in 1953 he played an important part in the removal of the dictator's hated hatchet man, Lavrentiy Beria, and was rewarded with the post of Defence Minister. He died in 1974.

Zhukov was a tough-minded military commander who stood up to the Soviet dictator. However, his story is not all heroic. He was never afraid to sacrifice his soldiers in order to secure a victory. He was generally brusque and coarse and was not averse to threatening his own generals with execution. Nevertheless, he did save the Soviet people in their hour of need.

53. THE T-34 TANK WAS A DECISIVE WEAPON FOR STALIN

The T-34 tank had only just started production when Hitler invaded the Soviet Union in June 1941. However, despite its appearance in relatively low quantities German generals were immediately impressed by its performance and loudly extolled its virtues. Indeed for many experts it would soon become the best tank of the Second World War.

So what was so remarkable about it? Just about everything, actually. To begin with its special design feature was heavily sloped armour, which made it difficult to knock out. Furthermore, its 76-mm gun was a highly effective weapon, particularly in the early years of the war. It was easy to manoeuvre and did not get bogged down in heavy mud or snow – pretty useful in Russia! Moreover, its simple design meant it was easy to mass-produce and repair. The Germans were so enamoured of the tank that any captured ones were immediately repainted and put to good use in their own army.

Due to dislocation caused by the rapid enemy advance production of the tank didn't get into full swing until the latter half of 1942. Stalingrad, though, remained a major production centre and, amazingly, in the battle there the tractor factory continued to roll out T-34s even as the fighting raged on around them.

The T-34 was to play a decisive role in the crucial battles of Stalingrad and Kursk (May 1943). In the final analysis, however, it was sheer numbers that overwhelmed the invader. By the end of the war over 80,000 had been manufactured, making it the most produced tank of the Second World War.

54. GOEBBELS DEMANDS TOTAL WAR

Josef Goebbels was the least likely of all the Nazi leaders. He was rather unprepossessing being quite short and walking with a pronounced limp due to a deformed right foot. He hardly fitted, therefore, into the category of your idealised Aryan. On the other hand, he was one of the best-educated and most intelligent members of Hitler's cabal. He had gained a doctorate from the University of Heidelberg in 1921, but it was his astute insight into the workings of the human mind that meant that he was well suited to running the Nazi Party propaganda machine.

To begin with Goebbels had been a fierce critic of Hitler's leadership of the party. However, at the Bamberg conference in 1926 he had been won over and thereafter offered the Führer his complete loyalty and devotion. Soon after the Nazis came to office in January 1933 Goebbels was rewarded with the position of Minister for Propaganda and Enlightenment. He soon showed his abilities by seizing control of all media outlets to get the Nazi message across. His greatest success prior to the war was to build up the image of the Nazi leader as an all-seeing, all-knowing genius. Historians have termed this 'the Hitler Myth'.

During the early years of the war Goebbels had found it easy to perpetuate this image of Hitler. Swift victories in Poland and France seemed to confirm all he was saying. However, failure to knock out Britain and setbacks in Russia began to tarnish the image. Defeat at Stalingrad presented the regime with an acute problem. Hitler and Goebbels had raised the German people's expectations of a victory there. Instead, the opposite had occurred, raising doubts about the government's honesty and competence. The 'Hitler Myth' had been fatally undermined. Not only had Hitler been directly responsible for the calamity, but also the German people suddenly realised that the war was perhaps lost.

With Hitler retreating into the shadows Goebbels more and more became the main face of the regime. He had always been good at making speeches and he now had the task of telling the nation that the war at home could not now carry on as before. Until Stalingrad Germany had still continued to turn out luxury goods and many sections of society had not been fully mobilised. Now all that had to change. If Germany was to have any chance of holding back the vast Soviet armies now heading in their direction the whole of German society and its economy needed to be mobilised for the war effort.

On the 18 February 1943 before a selected audience in the Sportpalast, Goebbels made his most famous speech: 'Do you want total war' he cried. 'Yes!' screamed back the crowd. 'Do you want a war more radical and total than anything you can imagine today?' 'Yes!' screamed the people again. Then, referring to the need for full mobilisation against the Russian hordes, he unfurled a historic slogan: 'And storm, break loose!'

The German people now understood what lay ahead for them.

55. Albert Speer Performs a Miracle

Albert Speer was an ambitious architect who worked his way up into the highest echelon of the Nazi regime. He ingratiated himself with Hitler and during the war was given the position of Minister of Armaments. The task of transforming German war production was one he set about with great zeal and efficiency and resulted in a remarkable turnaround.

It would be unfair to describe Speer as fully subscribing to the Nazi belief system. There is no evidence that he was anti-Semitic, but like many at the time he joined the party for personal advancement. He was a talented architect who first came to Hitler's notice with his design for the Nuremberg rally in 1933. Hitler took a special interest in architecture and the two men soon developed a close working relationship.

Speer eventually became Hitler's Chief Architect and was a regular visitor to his mountain retreat at Berchtesgaden. The two would spend hours together poring over designs of massive buildings, which Hitler intended would one day make up the centre of a new grandiose Berlin. If ever Hitler had a friend then Speer was this. The dictator commissioned Speer to create a new stadium for the Nuremberg rallies and a new chancellery. The construction of the latter Speer completed within a year by utilising shift work, working twenty-four hours round the clock.

His impressive organisational abilities must have influenced Hitler in appointing him as Minister of Armaments in February 1942. Speer was reluctant at first but the Führer was adamant. It turned out to be an inspired choice.

German armaments production prior to 1942 had been pitifully low in comparison with the Allies. This was partly to do with the disorganisation and fragmented nature of the Nazi state, but also the fact that the population and economy had not been fully mobilised. Speer approached the problem with a fresh mind and as one of his subordinates later noted, he didn't know what was possible and what was impossible and sometimes even performed the impossible!

The key to his success was the centralisation of all war production in himself with a central planning committee. He arranged for the factories to make single products and got the experts rather than the civil servants to supervise departments. Even in 1944 amid intensive Allied bombing production continued to increase exponentially. A few figures will suffice to give the reader a flavour. In the period from 1941 to 1944 tank production rose from 4,800 to 27,300 and aircraft production from 11,800 to 39,800. By the second half of 1944 there was sufficient equipment to provide for 270 army divisions even though there were just over half that number actually in the field.

It was an incredible achievement and Hitler was so delighted that he once greeted him with a 'Heil Speer'. But the reality was that it had come far too late and merely delayed the inevitable.

56. Manstein Stabilises the Front at Kharkov

Field-Marshal Fritz Erich von Manstein has been rated as the greatest German military strategist of the Second World War. His understanding of modern tank warfare and the art of thrust and manoeuvre was almost unrivalled. His cool, calm exterior was rarely ruffled. With his quick, clear mind he was noted for his speedy decision making.

In the war against France in 1940 it had been his idea to launch the surprise attack through the Ardennes which had split the Allies and caused the British to retreat hastily back to Dunkirk. In the war in the Soviet Union his northern thrust had rapidly brought German armies to the gates of Leningrad. When posted to the southern front in the summer of 1942 he carried out a successful campaign that had crushed all Soviet resistance in the Crimea. It was little wonder that he was put forward three times for the post of Chief of Staff of the army. As Hitler held that post himself this suggestion was firmly rejected!

Although Manstein had failed to relieve Stalingrad Hitler still esteemed the general and had much need of his services. His allotted task in early 1943 was to stabilise the southern front as the debacle of Stalingrad unfolded. Soviet armies were pressing and there was a danger of collapse.

He first of all successfully extricated German forces that had ventured down into the Caucasus the previous year and were in danger of being cut off. He then pulled his forces back behind the River Mius, which was a distance of some 300 miles. This manoeuvre clearly aided the German recovery. Not only did it give the German armies a respite, but it also allowed time for fresh forces to join him; in particular, a whole SS Panzer corps had recently arrived from France and the local Luftwaffe (German Air Force) had been sent reinforcements.

Manstein was helped now by Stalin's erroneous strategy of pressing his forces forward all along the front. Soviet armies in the south were becoming dangerously overstretched and spread out far too thinly. Since Stalingrad they had travelled hundreds of miles in severe winter conditions and were short of supplies. The German general now saw his chance for a counterstroke.

Kharkov lay to the north of the River Mius. It had been recently recaptured by Soviet forces and the Soviet high command believed that by advancing rapidly they could surround and cut off German forces to the south. Manstein now launched his surprise counter-offensive trapping Russian spearheads south of the city. After fierce fighting Kharkov itself soon fell to the Germans. As many as 90,000 Soviet soldiers were lost in the campaign. Manstein's 'mobile defence' operation has since become a textbook model for military planners.

It was a bitter defeat for the Russians. They had underestimated the strength of the German Army, which remained a fearsome behemoth. However, Manstein's victory only brought a temporary respite. The whole front was creaking and further German setbacks were in the offing.

57. The Dambusters Didn't Bust All the Dams

The Ruhr area can be considered the industrial heart of Germany. The British had the idea that if they could destroy the dams, which controlled the rivers that flowed through the region, they could strike a significant blow at the enemy war effort. The dilemma was how to go about it. Normal bombing from above was too inaccurate and would be unlikely to cause a breach even if a direct hit was scored. Somehow the dams would need to be struck from the side to have any impact.

The British government gave the task of finding a solution to Dr Barnes Wallis. He had already designed the Wellesley and Wellington bombers with the latter becoming a mainstay of the British bomber force. After several experiments Wallis decided that a special portly-shaped 'bouncing' bomb would be needed. This would permit the bombs to get over the torpedo nets before striking the dams, after which the bombs would sink down and explode at the base of the dams. It meant it would be a tricky operation for the bomber crews as they would need to come in very low but then pull up quickly to avoid colliding with the dam parapet.

A squadron of experienced flyers was quickly assembled, which was soon named 617 Squadron. In charge of organising the attack was Air-Vice Marshall the Hon. Ralph Cochrane. Specially converted Lancaster bombers would now be required to cater for the new 'upkeep' bomb, as it was now called. Struts or arms came down each side of the fuselage to carry the 7-foot-long cylindrical bomb. A small motor was attached to it to enable the bomb to be spinning backwards (at around 500 revolutions a minute) when it hit the water. In addition to these technical requirements getting the bombers to approach at the right height and speed would take a lot of practice.

After three months of trial runs across mountainous areas in Scotland and Wales the crews were ready. On the night of 16–17 May 1943 three formations left England. The dams were well defended, so not only did they have to navigate precisely in the dark but they also had to endure a baptism of fire. The first group of nine successfully reached the Möhne Dam and after three attempts caused a huge breach allowing 330 million tons of water to be unleashed into the valley below. Similar destruction was caused on the Eder dam. Under increasing fog attempts made on the Sorpe and Ennepe dams proved ineffectual. This was a disappointment for the squadron as the destruction of the former dam in particular would have been far more cataclysmic. Of the nineteen planes that left eleven returned home with fifty-six crew members lost.

In the aftermath of the raid some factories and land were ruined, but by the end of June full electricity and water production was restored. No follow-up raids were launched and so the final result was disappointing. Nevertheless, it was a huge psychological blow on the Reich.

58. A German Army Is Deserted in the Desert

After the defeat of El Alamein (Fact 50) in November 1942 the German General Erwin Rommel had managed an orderly withdrawal all the way back to Tunisia. It was a mighty achievement given that his forces were being constantly harassed from the air and on the ground by British forces under Bernard Montgomery advancing from Egypt. Rommel's problems were compounded by the landing of largely American forces in north-west Africa (Operation Torch) in the autumn. He was therefore being squeezed in a vice with Allied forces coming from both East and West. Common sense now dictated that Rommel should beat a retreat back to the Italian Peninsula. Adolf Hitler, however, had other ideas!

The German dictator was aware that his Italian ally, Mussolini, was facing a potentially disastrous situation. If the Allies managed to take control of Tunisia, then they would be only a stone's throw from Italy itself with invasion surely in the offing. With this in mind Hitler decided to prop up the Axis forces in North Africa by sending in over 100,000 extra German troops to support Rommel. For the German commander this must have made no sense as Hitler was now effectively pouring men and arms into a lost situation. In addition, the Führer was offering him troops that he had steadfastly refused to give him only a few months earlier before the Battle of El Alamein.

As mentioned before, Operation Torch had seen the landings of over 107,000 American and British forces in French Vichy-controlled Morocco and Algeria. Their task was to co-ordinate with Montgomery in the east and seize Tunisia. If the Allies were feeling confident about the developing situation they soon received a rude awakening.

Raw, untested, American troops moving forward into Tunisia were given a severe mauling at the battle of the Kasserine Pass. Rommel's surprise offensive had shown up the Allied lack of preparation and lamentably poor liaison. In the end Rommel pulled back due to lack of fuel and food supplies.

Within a month, however, the situation had altered. The Axis forces had lost control of the air and found themselves squeezed on two fronts. General George Patton ('Old blood and guts') leading the American II corps scored a victory at El Guettar in the west while Monty leading the British Eighth Army to the south-east forced a German retreat at the Mareth Line.

The Allies were also helped by a secret weapon. Ultra, from Bletchley Park, kept the Allied commanders informed of Axis convoys from Italy. It permitted the Allies, with pinpoint accuracy, to sink those Axis ships carrying arms and equipment. Rather craftily only food convoys were allowed through. The Germans were convinced that Italian spies were to blame.

Constantly battered from the skies and lacking fuel and equipment, it could only be a matter of time before the Axis troops called it a day. Eventually, in May, 230,000 German and Italian troops surrendered. For Hitler it was a disaster to match Stalingrad. For the Allies the next stop was Sicily.

59. Kursk Was a Battle That Hitler Couldn't Win

Imagine, if you will, a huge bulge jutting out into the middle of the German front line in Russia. It measures 120 miles wide and 90 miles deep. In the centre of the pocket lies the city of Kursk, once famed for its nightingales and bird-singing competitions. Very soon the area would only ring out to the deafening decibels of war.

The Kursk salient was in fact a recent legacy of the Soviet Army's reckless dash forward after the capitulation of Stalingrad in February 1943. The German front had eventually held leaving some Russian forces in a somewhat exposed position. Clearly a German counter-attack from north and south into the bottleneck of the salient would result in a huge Nazi victory. Manstein was keen to strike as early as March. Hitler demurred. Although he craved a success which would wipe out the memory of Stalingrad, he ordered a delay in which further forces could be brought to the front, including the new heavyweight Tiger tank. This was a massive beast weighing 54 tons and far heavier than anything the Soviets could field. Unfortunately, only twelve a week were being produced. Hitler, however, pinned his hopes on this tank being the key to victory.

While the Nazi dictator delayed the Soviets rapidly set about building up their forces in the salient. Stalin knew of the impending attack from spies and other sources. Instead of launching an offensive he now heeded the advice of Zhukov to go for 'defence in depth'. The Russian Army would absorb the attack and with forces held in reserve launch a massive counter-attack.

When Hitler's long-expected attack (Operation Citadel) came in July his forces were confronting an almost impossible gauntlet. Soviet defence lines stretched back

150 miles and over a million mines had been laid. One and a half million men had been stuffed into the pocket with a further half a million in reserve. In addition there were 20,000 artillery pieces lined up and waiting. Hitler's Reich could barely match these numbers.

The Germans were relying on the fighting prowess of their finest SS Panzer divisions to break through. In the event the outcome was predictable. In the north Field Marshal Walther Model's armies could only manage an advance of 6 miles after five days, while in the south General Hermann Hoth's forces gave up after penetrating 9 miles.

Only in one area, at Prokhorovka in the south, did an SS Panzer force break through. Zhukov rushed a reserve Soviet tank force to the area. Both combatants had around 900 tanks and fought an epic battle at close quarters. The engagement raged for eight hours and has gone down as the largest tank battle in history. One German officer described it as the 'veritable death ride of the 4th Panzer Army'. Both sides suffered terrible losses but there was still no German breakthrough.

With a victory no longer in sight Hitler called off Operation Citadel. Zhukov's devastating counter-offensive was about to be unleashed, which would drive Nazi forces out of Russia.

60. 'Mincemeat Is Swallowed Rod, Line and Sinker!'

As noted before, after the capture of Tunisia in May 1943 the obvious next stop for the Allies was Sicily. However, taking the Italian island could be a costly exercise if the Axis forces had it well defended. Two men in London working on a small committee dealing with subterfuge and double agents hatched a plan to deceive the Axis powers about where the Allied armies would now strike. It became known as Operation Mincemeat.

The two men in question were Charles Cholmondeley and Ewen Montagu, who worked on the Twenty Committee (after the Roman numerals for double cross –'XX'). Their idea was that a body with important documents would be found floating in the sea off the coast of Spain after an imaginary plane crash. The documents would make out that the Allies were intent on attacking Sardinia and Greece next *not* Sicily. Spain was sympathetic to the Axis cause and any papers found would inevitably end up in Berlin. The problem was this: how do you convince the Germans that the documents are genuine?

The body of a deceased vagrant was found for the task. His new synthetic identity was that of a Major W. Martin, who was attached to Allied headquarters in North Africa. The key document was a letter from the vice-chief of the Imperial General Staff, which set out the supposed future 'plans' in the Mediterranean. The false documents were placed in a briefcase and attached to his belt. He was given false identity papers and letters from various people in his imaginary life including a fiancée. Crucially for the deception, not all the documents were in perfect order. For example, his ID card was a replacement for one he had 'carelessly' lost and his pass for the Allied HQ had expired. The body in its uniform was placed in a canister and filled with dry ice and despatched in a submarine, whose crew then left the body floating off the south-west coast of Spain. The Allies now awaited events.

Sure enough after a short while a Spanish fishing fleet returned to port with an unusual haul. The contents of the briefcase were secretly ferreted to the German embassy in Madrid, where a copy of the documents was made and hurriedly sent on to Berlin. Everything was then returned apparently unopened to the British attaché in the Spanish capital. Goebbels, the Nazi Propaganda Minister, was decidedly doubtful about the documents but Hitler declared himself convinced of their veracity. Decrypts from Bletchley confirmed that the Führer had taken the bait. A triumphant message was sent to Churchill: 'Mincemeat is swallowed rod, line and sinker!'

The deception worked a treat. Sicily was not turned into a fortress. Instead defences were bulked up in Sardinia and Greece. Amazingly, Hitler even moved panzer divisions to Greece from France and the Russian front, where they were sorely needed. When the Allies duly invaded the island in July they had an unexpectedly easy time of it.

61. Italy Was Not Such a Soft Underbelly

After their victories in North Africa, the Allies were intent on the conquest of Italy. Churchill had convinced the Americans that Italy was the 'soft underbelly' of Europe. It would soon be rolled up and the Allies could then proceed to launch offensives into France and assist the Soviet Union in the Balkans. This policy suited Britain, which wanted to protect its imperial interests in the Mediterranean (Malta, Gibraltar and the Suez Canal) and also avoid heavy losses which might be the result of launching a second front with a direct cross-Channel invasion of France. For the moment the Americans agreed but Stalin, the Soviet leader saw it as a strategy to leave the Soviet Union to do most of the fighting.

Operation Husky, the codename for the invasion of Sicily, started on 10 July 1943. The American general George Patton landed his forces on the south of the island and the British general Montgomery in command of the Eighth Army landed on the south-eastern tip. Limited Axis troops were slowly driven back. Montgomery found it hard going in the mountains on the east coast where resistance was tough, while the American General Patton raced across the island in the west and reached the north-east coast before him – much to Montgomery's chagrin!

Italian dictator Benito Mussolini now found his position untenable. His own Fascist Grand Council voted him down and the Italian king dismissed him. General Badoglio was appointed Prime Minister and set about secretly negotiating terms with the Allies while proclaiming his loyalty to Germany. These discussions with the Allies were long and protracted and the Germans suspected some treachery was going on. Almost inevitably, just prior to the Allied invasion of the Italian mainland in

September, the Germans swept down and took control of the whole of Italy.

Operation Avalanche saw a double landing. Montgomery landed in Reggio on the toe of Italy while the Americans under General Mark Clark landed further north at Salerno, just south of Naples. The intention was to trap German armies in a pincer. However, this time Hitler's forces under Field Marshall Albert Kesselring put up such fierce resistance that the Americans almost considered re-embarkation. Nevertheless, the Allies eventually won through and Kesselring pulled his forces back north of Naples.

This first part had been relatively easy but the avowed aim of driving on to Rome proved much more testing. The German commander soon showed himself to be a master of defensive operations. By using the mountainous terrain and rivers that straddled the peninsula he was able to create defence lines that proved incredibly difficult to break. As winter set in rain, sleet and snow caused the Allied advance to grind to a freezing and muddy halt. Taking Italy was going to be a slow and painful process.

The Americans were becoming sceptical of Churchill's Mediterranean strategy. General Mark Clark summed it up when he noted that Italy was less of a 'soft underbelly' but more of a 'tough old gut'!

62. MUSSOLINI IS SAVED IN AN AUDACIOUS RESCUE

After the deposal of Benito Mussolini in July 1943 (Fact 61) Hitler was determined to rescue his old chum. He may have been a complete chump but the Führer retained a lingering respect for his old comrade in arms. SS Obersturmbannführer Otto Skorzeny, who headed a small special commando outfit, was selected for the task. The new Italian government had imprisoned the dictator in a secret location and it was not until the end of August that the Germans gleaned that Mussolini was being held in a hotel in a mountain retreat called Gran Sasso.

In view of its inaccessibility and the rough terrain gliders were used carrying in total 108 paratroopers. When the operation went ahead on 13 May complete success was achieved. Luckily, bloodshed was avoided as the Germans had brought an Italian general along who persuaded the guards to lay down their arms. Mussolini was then whisked off to Rome in a tiny Fieseler Storch. There was only room for two people including the pilot, but Skorzeny managed to cram himself in, intent on taking his prize to the Führer himself. The heavily overloaded plane proved a hair-raising flight.

Mussolini was immediately taken to Hitler's command post on the Eastern front. The German leader delightedly told Skorzeny 'Today you have carried out a mission which will go down in history.' Despite the congratulations Hitler later declared himself 'extraordinarily disappointed' by the broken-down appearance and defeated look of his old ally. Perhaps unwillingly Mussolini was then despatched back to northern Italy to head a puppet regime called the Salò Republic.

63. There Was a Bad and a Good Goering

Hermann Goering was the baddie. He had gained fame as an air ace in the First World War before joining the Nazi Party in 1922. Like many he was inspired by Hitler's message that Versailles should be torn up and Germany made great once again. His loyalty to Hitler was rewarded with the job of Luftwaffe chief and was effectively deputy Führer. However, he was also responsible for setting up the notorious Gestapo and establishing a reign of terror when the Nazis came to power in 1933.

His brother, however, was quite a contrast. Although the brothers had grown up together in a fairy tale castle in Bavaria, they turned out quite differently. Albert was a humanitarian and abhorred the Nazi Party with its brutality and anti-Semitism. When the Nazis took over in Austria in 1938 he worked tirelessly to get exit visas for his Jewish friends. Likewise, later on while Export Director of the Czech firm Skoda he helped Jewish workers to escape and even turned a blind eye to the resistance. The remarkable fact is that he often requested (and received!) his brother's signature releasing Jewish workers for him. The Gestapo had arrest warrants out for him several times but Hermann always intervened to save his brother.

After the war Hermann was found guilty at the Nuremberg trials and committed suicide before facing the hangman. Albert, unfortunately, spent two years in gaol before the Allied authorities believed his story. He died in a penniless state in 1966. Those he saved have never forgotten his kindness.

64. Dönitz Calls It a Day in the Atlantic

Grand Admiral Karl Dönitz was in charge of the German U-boats that were rampaging across the Atlantic and sinking vital supplies bound for Britain courtesy of her American ally. In the first few months of 1943 things appeared to be going very well for the Nazi commander. He now had 300 submarines that could almost range at will and were enjoying something of a turkey shoot with 108 merchant ships sunk in March alone. The Führer was delighted.

Within a few months, however, the situation was to change dramatically in favour of the Allies. America and Britain had to overcome the U-boat problem if they were to challenge Hitler in the west. There was not going to be a cross-Channel invasion of France if massive quantities of troops and supplies could not be safely ferried across the Atlantic. Clearing the Atlantic was a priority.

So what caused the change about in fortunes? To begin the Allies were able to overcome the problem of the 'Black Gap'. This was a vast area in the centre of the Atlantic which could not be covered by Allied aircraft. New long-range Liberator aircraft with shortwave radar at last enabled the Allies to cover this space. In addition, planes were also able to hunt down submarines at night thanks to the Leigh Light, which was a powerful marine searchlight. Once the U-boat had been discovered it could be despatched with a lethal depth charge.

Improvements in radar meant that even periscopes could be spotted at some distance away. This was the result of the creation of the cavity magnetron and centimetric radar. A further innovation that was starting to prove effective was the use of special support groups of destroyers whose purpose was solely to hunt down and destroy U-boats. With the benefit of radar developments these hunting groups proved evermore effective. An added weapon in this area was 'Huff-Duff' (HF/DF), which was a high frequency direction finder that enabled the short wave messages between U-boats to be detected. Once the U-boat had been located depth charges could be used to bring it to the surface. A development on this idea was the 'hedgehog', which was a multiple bomb launcher fired from the front of destroyers – it sent out twenty-four small bombs each fitted with contact fuses. Only a direct hit with an enemy submarine produced the desired explosion.

The final icing on the cake was the work carried out at Bletchley. Two U-boats were boarded enabling code books to be seized and the German naval codes to be broken. This permitted convoys to be rerouted and for individual submarines to be hunted down.

Already by May the writing was on the wall for the Germans. In that month alone forty U-boats were sunk with a further 141 lost by the end of the year. Such a high loss rate was unacceptable and Dönitz was forced to withdraw his U-boats in the Atlantic.

Hitler realised all too well that very soon the Allies would be able launch a second front.

65. CHURCHILL SETS EUROPE ALIGHT

Winston Churchill was keen to strike back at the Nazi regime immediately after the fall of France in June 1940. So in the following month an organisation was set up called the Special Operations Executive (SOE) whose sole mission was, in the great man's words, 'to set Europe ablaze'. The way this was to be achieved was set out in its founding charter, which stated that action was to be 'by way of subversion and sabotage'. Its work was to be entirely secret and its existence was never acknowledged by the government.

The tentacles of this new organisation were to stretch into almost every part of Axis-occupied Europe. There was a huge mixture of operatives within the organisation – from upper-class, Cambridge-educated officers to peasants and prostitutes. Indeed, the SOE was not above using the underworld for operations. In addition, women were sent into front-line duties and as many as fifty were later dropped into France. Training meant going through a 'series of sieves' at the end of which only the most hardy and resourceful were selected.

A brief overview of the operations will give the reader an idea of the scale of the endeavours. France and Yugoslavia were given greatest attention, but no country was neglected. Norway, for example, received a stream of agents and supplies during its period of Nazi occupation. The most spectacular operation was against the Norsk Hydro Plant, where heavy water was being manufactured for Germany's atomic bomb project. In February 1943 agents managed to enter the plant through a poorly guarded side entrance. After blowing up a section of the plant the Norwegians escaped over a snowy plateau. Incredibly, despite being chased by 12,000 German troops they managed to avoid capture. Later on, a ferry containing a heavy water consignment for the Reich was blown up, too. It marked the end of Nazi attempts to build a nuclear bomb.

In what is today the Czech Republic, Reinhard Heydrich had set himself up as Governor General. You may recall that he was a leading light of the SS and responsible for setting up the Holocaust. Heydrich's rule was especially brutal and he was a tempting target. In May 1943 two specially trained Czech agents were parachuted in and in broad daylight 'the blond beast' was gunned down in a Prague street. Alas, the agents did not escape and Nazi retribution was ferocious. Nevertheless, it showed that nowhere in Europe was safe for the Nazi occupiers.

France, of course, received the most attention with 500 agents being parachuted in. It had its own special division called 'F' section under the control of a certain Major Maurice Buckmaster. The support given to the resistance there created a constant problem for the Nazi authorities and the coordinated sabotage efforts at the time of the Normandy landings proved especially effective.

SOE was not decisive in the war, nor was it always successful. However, it did important work and gave vital assistance to resistance networks across Europe.

66. The Chinese Get Help via the Hump

The war in China has often been a neglected part of the history of the Second World War in the West. This may be because of the fact that Western forces had very little involvement there and therefore not a great deal of understanding of the conflict. Then there is the complication of the confused political situation and finally, of course, the difficulty of Chinese names!

For the Chinese hostilities began much earlier than in Europe. Already in 1931 the Imperial Japanese Army had seized a part of northern China called Manchuria. However, hostilities didn't really heat up until 1937 with the Marco Polo Bridge Incident when Japan decided on a full-scale invasion of China. The Massacre of Nanking when 300,000 Chinese died marked the beginning of a particularly gruesome conflict. After Pearl Harbour in December 1941 China formally declared war on Japan and the Axis powers and became one of the Allied powers.

The Japanese in 1937 believed that they would have an easy time of it and even boasted that they would be able to conquer China within three months. The reason for this is that China was in a state of civil war with the communists under Mao Zedong on the one side and the nationalists under Chiang Kai-shek on the other. In addition to this, there were various warlords who controlled vast areas of the country. In modern terms it would be called a failed state. Nevertheless, all sides eventually agreed to bury the hatchet and to fight as a united front against the invader.

By 1941 the Chinese nationalist government (or Kuomintang) was still putting up fierce resistance although lacking the military capacity to launch large-scale offensives that could drive the enemy out of their country. By 1942 the Japanese controlled large areas of the north and coastal areas of China, however they were finding it difficult to make further headway and occasionally even suffered defeats. As a result of this the Japanese resorted to using various nasties not permitted by the Hague conventions; for example, chemical weapons were employed in 1938 and later on a variety of pathogens were deployed, such as bubonic plague, cholera, typhoid and dysentery. The war was leaving a trail of utter misery and devastation.

The Americans were keen to offer assistance to the Chinese in any way possible. The problem was how to get help to them as the coastal areas were mostly occupied. At first the main route to China was via the Burma Road that led through from India. This was cut with the Japanese invasion of Burma itself in 1942. After this the Americans flew sorties over the Himalayas, which became known as the Hump. By 1945 they had delivered 650,000 tons of supplies to the nationalists but in the process almost 600 planes were lost on the hazardous flight.

Nevertheless, these supplies provided vital succour for the Chinese and meant over a million Japanese troops continued to be tied down who could have been used elsewhere.

67. A Countess Runs an Escape Line

By 1943 there was a myriad of escape lines across Western Europe set up to assist anybody considered a refugee from Nazi justice – they could be downed pilots or escapers from prisoner of war camps. Typically, an Allied pilot who had bailed out in northern France would be kept in a safe house until he could be given safe passage to the Spanish border. From there he would be taken over the Pyrenees and thence to Gibraltar. Fascist Spain was officially neutral at the time.

The men and women who ran these escape lines often showed incredible heroism and the story of Mary Lindell is just one example. Mary was brought up in England and served in the First World War as a nurse. She received rewards for gallantry and dedication to the wounded from both the French and Russian governments. After the war she married a certain Count de Milleville, with whom she had three children.

With the defeat and occupation of France in 1940 Mary lost no time in assisting escapers, and the whole family took part in the enterprise. As a result of her activities she was captured by the Gestapo and banged up in Fresnes Prison for nine months. Her son, Maurice, was also captured, tortured and imprisoned. After this she fled Paris and escaped back to England.

Mary was determined to carry on with her work, however. In 1942 after completing training with M19 (tasked with helping escape lines) she returned to the town of Ruffec (in western France) to set up a new network called the Marie-Claire line. The line was active with immediate effect and she was able to assist two British commandos who had recently carried out a raid on Bordeaux. Unfortunately, around this time she suffered appalling injuries when she was deliberately rammed off her bicycle by a collaborator's car. She was taken to hospital by fellow resistance workers but had to be stretchered down to a cellar when the Gestapo came looking for her. Afterwards she insisted on carrying on her work despite not being fully recovered.

As 1943 drew on there was a steady stream of Allied aircrews seeking assistance. However, getting them out across the Pyrenees into Spain was becoming increasingly difficult due to heightened German security measures. One day while waiting at Pau station for four 'parcels' she was arrested by the SD (Secret Police) and placed on a train for Paris. She managed to jump from the train but her guards loosed off two shots, which went into her face and head. Ironically, her life was then saved by a German surgeon.

After her recovery it was decided not to execute her but to send her to Ravensbrück concentration camp. In April 1945, determined and indomitable, she at last walked free.

At the time of her capture there were 160 airmen waiting in safe houses. It is not clear how many 'evaders' Mary Lindell saved but it is reckoned to be several hundred.

68. The Japanese Military Believed in Face Slapping

The military creed of Japan went back to the days of the samurai when the warriors of yore were guided by a chivalric code of bushido. However, this 'spirit of bushido' was exploited and doctored by the regime and embedded into the wartime Japanese Army. War was presented as purifying and death a duty. To die for the emperor would be an honour.

Discipline throughout the army was strictly enforced. Any orders that were misunderstood or not carried out correctly were met with face slapping. This permeated down through the ranks and for Allied prisoners of war who misunderstood instructions on a daily basis face slapping was then a frequent occurrence.

As all Japanese soldiers were expected to fight and die in an honourable way surrender was out of the question and was considered a disgrace; hence when European soldiers gave in seemingly almost without a fight the Japanese soldier had nothing but disdain for them. These prisoners, it was believed, owed a debt to their captors that could never be repaid. The resulting brutal treatment knew no limits and torture and beheadings were not unknown.

The 'spirit of bushido' meant that Japanese forces would accept any orders to fight to the death. In the closing years of the war Japanese pilots were expected to sacrifice themselves in kamikaze fashion against the advancing American armada. In addition, when defeat and disgrace loomed a Japanese officer might choose hara-kiri to atone.

This all contributed to make the Japanese Army a fearsome military machine.

69. A Death Railway Is Completed Ahead of Schedule

After the fall of Burma in mid-1942 the Japanese were determined to continue their offensive by attacking British India. The problem was that supplying their forces by sea was no longer an option due to the American victory at Midway Island. Supplies and men would have to come overland via Thailand and across Burma itself. A railway would need to be built which in total would stretch for 258 miles. The Japanese were not short of workers to carry this out as they could use Asian civilian labour and Allied prisoners of war taken in Hong Kong, Singapore and elsewhere.

Work began in the autumn of 1942 and initially the conditions were bearable for workers. However, with the arrival of the monsoon season conditions rapidly worsened. British and other Allied forces were sometimes made to march all day before being forced to set up camp in torrential rain. With little protection from the elements the main task in such circumstances was survival. This was made all the more difficult by Japanese maltreatment of the prisoners, which included harsh punishments and long hours of work. The rations were poor and many men ended up with beriberi due to a deficiency of vitamin B in the rice diet. On top of this the prisoners soon acquired various other diseases such as malaria, scabies, dysentery, typhus, smallpox and even spinal meningitis! Inevitably, the death rate remained high.

In early 1943 the Japanese decided that they needed to bring in more prisoners to hasten the work. In addition, they now ratcheted up the pressure on the men and 'speedo' became the order of the day. Many who were clearly sick were forced to work and no more than 10 per cent of prisoners were allowed to stay in the 'hospitals'.

Those who stayed back in camp were given reduced rations to encourage the others. This treatment, of course, left the ranks decimated. Two British work parties sent out from Singapore in April 1943 were treated in this way. Only 3,200 men returned out of an original force of 10,000.

Hellfire Pass in Burma has gone down in history as the worst example of the demands exacted on the prisoners. Without proper tools the men had to hack through sheer rock in order to create a cutting. Japanese treatment was excessively harsh with sixty-nine men being beaten to death, and many more dying of disease, starvation and exhaustion. It is all too easy to understand why the Burma Railway was dubbed the 'Death Railway'.

Various bridges had to be constructed by the prisoners. Famously a film was made in 1957 by David Lean entitled *A Bridge on the River Kwai* starring Alec Guinness.

In the end the railway was finished three months ahead of schedule in October 1943. But the cost had been enormous. Something like 90,000 Asian workers and over 12,000 Allied prisoners had died.

The Japanese never did invade India and just over a year later the railway was abandoned.

70. Many British Prisoners Preferred Knitting to Escaping

While many British soldiers taken prisoner by the Japanese had a hard time of it, those captured in Europe had it easy by comparison. Early on in the war the latter would be greeted by the phrase 'For you the war is over'. Officers and men were then separated out. Ordinary privates would be sent to Stalags where they were usually expected to work. Officers, on the other hand, were sent to Oflags where they were given a life of enforced leisure. How to fill that time became a problem.

It is a surprising fact that knitting was one of the more popular pastimes for many officers. This is not to say that this was their sole activity; others indulged in making models of aircraft or railways while some took up painting and drawing. Reading and self-improvement were also popular and more than a million books were left behind by Allied prisoners in 1945. You could even take special degree courses and it is estimated that 17,000 exams were sat during the war. The theatre was also popular with some men controversially taking on some of the female roles.

Sport became an important part of camp life. The Red Cross generously supplied tens of thousands of footballs, tennis balls and boxing gloves. Another 'sport' was teasing the German guards. The prisoners called themselves 'Kriegies' and the Germans were dubbed 'Goons'. 'Goon-baiting' was one way of passing the time, especially during 'Appells'. The Germans regularly held these in order to disrupt escape plans or to discover illegal radios etc.

Another hobby practised was trying to escape. It is reckoned, however, that only around 5 per cent of internees were habitual escape artists and the majority of their attempts failed – most headed for Switzerland or the German ports but very few made it there due a lack of German and general wherewithal. Well-forged documents did not guarantee your survival, especially when Nazi security forces were scouring the countryside for you.

Famously, some did manage to carry out a home run. Colditz Castle was supposed to be escape proof but Airey Neave and his Dutch companion brazenly walked straight out dressed as German army officers. Pat Reid and three fellow prisoners managed to get out through a narrow flue. Each of them was carrying a small suitcase with the idea that once out they would appear to be foreign workers. The trick worked and they all made it all the way to Switzerland.

The 'Great Escape' of March 1944 took place in a Stalag south-east of Berlin. This time it was achieved using tunnels. Rather inventively they built three named 'Tom', 'Dick' and 'Harry'. The idea was that if the Germans discovered one tunnel they would stop searching. A grand total of seventy-six prisoners got out through 'Harry', but unfortunately fifty of these were rounded up and executed by the Gestapo and only three made it back home.

Escape, then, was a risky business. No wonder many officer-class prisoners preferred to stay put and enjoy their knitting!

71. The Germans Reap the Whirlwind

In the early years of the war the German Luftwaffe was able to bomb other countries almost at will; for example, several cities in Holland, Britain and the Soviet Union were particularly devastated. However, when the tide of war began to turn it was inevitable the Allies would seek retribution. Sir Arthur 'Bomber' Harris, Chief of British Bomber Command, used a Jewish proverb to set out his stall: 'They have sowed the wind, now they will reap the whirlwind.'

To begin with attempts to hit Germany's industry proved something of a joke. A report in 1941 highlighted the fact that only a third of British bombs got within 5 miles of the target. German defences meant daytime bombers were forced to fly at a great height while those at night had difficulty identifying their targets. After his appointment in early 1942 Harris soon abandoned the idea of precision bombing and instead advocated the idea of 'Strategic' or 'Area' bombing at night. The hope was that deliberately hitting civilians would destroy morale as well as industrial output and just possibly the war could be won by bombing alone.

The Americans, however, took a different view and sent in bombing raids during the day. They were able to hit industrial targets more precisely but suffered horrific losses of around 20 per cent. In 1943 the Allies were able to launch increasingly heavy raids. The British bombing of Hamburg over three nights in July proved particularly devastating. Dry weather caused a massive firestorm resulting in over 40,000 German civilians being literally incinerated as temperatures rose to over 1,000 degrees Celsius in the city centre. But despite the fact that Germany and the Nazi regime were shaken, morale did not break.

Losses of Allied bomber crews over Germany remained high due to the lack of fighter protection. The Germans maintained a large fighter force forewarned by an effective radar defence system leaving Allied bombers at their mercy. However, all this changed at the beginning of 1944 when an American fighter, the Mustang P51, suddenly appeared in vast numbers over the skies of the Reich. With its larger fuel tank it was able to protect the Allied bombers right across Germany. Famously, Hermann Goering, the Luftwaffe Commander, initially refused to believe the first sightings as he feared it would spell doom for Germany in the air war. He was right. By March the German fighter force had been decimated and lost control of the skies forever.

It was now the turn of the Allies to be able to bomb at will. More precision bombing meant they were now able to target areas such as steel and synthetic oil production, which were reduced by as much as 80 per cent. Controversially, in February 1945 British bombers destroyed the undefended city of Dresden, leaving 25,000 civilians dead. Germany had truly reaped the whirlwind.

Bombing by itself did not win the war but it did strike at Germany's ability to maintain production. In the process 55,000 Allied pilots and perhaps half a million German civilians lost their lives.

72. A Bear Helps Wage War on the Nazis

A 6-foot bear is not something you expect to see on a battlefield, still less supplying ammunition to an artillery company. Incredibly, this actually happened. Some Polish soldiers adopted a bear cub and trained it up while it accompanied them on their tours of duty.

It all started in the spring of 1942. Polish troops who had been released from Soviet captivity found themselves stationed in Iran, and the men there decided to adopt a Syrian bear cub that had recently been orphaned. He was named Wojtek (pronounced *voytek*), which translates as 'joyful warrior'. At first he was fed on condensed milk out of a vodka bottle before graduating on to fruit, marmalade and honey. Unfortunately, as a youth he got into bad company, was led astray and ended up drinking beer and smoking (and eating) cigarettes. Beer soon became his favourite tipple – straight from the bottle, of course.

Wojtek became great mates with the unit, slept with them in the tents and enjoyed wrestling with them. He was trained to salute and liked travelling in the front of vehicles with his head hanging out the side causing consternation to all passers-by.

The Polish unit, the 22nd Artillery Supply Company, was under British jurisdiction and was posted to Palestine before going on to Egypt and Italy. However, British Army rules forbad animals being kept in camp, so Wojtek was made a private with a pay-book and serial number.

In 1944 the unit was posted to southern Italy, where it participated in the bloody battle of Monte Cassino. Wojtek was keen to play his full part and manfully set to by carrying heavy boxes of ammunition forward to the guns – apparently, he was unperturbed by the sound of gunfire. This image of a bear carrying howitzer ammunition soon became the emblem of the unit.

At the war's end Wojtek obtained a well-earned promotion to corporal before being assigned to Edinburgh Zoo. He was often visited by his old playmates, who would offer him cigarettes and sometimes jump in for a wrestle for old time's sake. He died in 1963 at the age of twenty-two.

Wojtek is remembered to this day. In 2013 Krakow city in Poland and Edinburgh City Council gave the go-ahead for the erection of bronze statues in his memory. To cap it all a film was made in 2011 that recorded his exploits.

Of course this is not the full story – merely the *bear* details! (I humbly beg for the reader's forbearance here.)

73. Himmler Was an Evil Fantasist

Heinrich Himmler is renowned for being Hitler's most ruthless and evil acolyte. He was in charge of all security forces including the SS and was directly responsible for the genocidal policies carried out in the concentration camps and elsewhere. Yet he was also imbued with a romanticised view of German history.

Nothing prepared the world for the emergence of this mass-murderer. His family background was a traditional stable one. His father was a teacher and tutored a member of the Bavarian royal family. Himmler was too young to participate in the First World War but felt the bitterness of many at Germany's defeat. After joining the Nazi Party he became one of Hitler's most loyal supporters. By 1929 he had worked his way up in the party to becoming head of the tiny SS, which at that time only numbered 280 men. The official task of the unit was to be Hitler's bodyguard, but Himmler soon expanded its role into a large elite force.

By the time the Nazis came to power in 1933 the SS had expanded to 50,000. In theory, they were still a subordinate part of the SA (Stormtroopers), but a year later the SS took part in the Night of the Long Knives, which effectively removed the SA as an obstacle to his ambitions. From now on Himmler expanded his powers inexorably. By 1936 he had taken full control of the Gestapo and all police and security forces across Germany. This included the notorious concentration camps. By the outbreak of war Himmler had also created a military wing called the Waffen SS, whose members became the most feared and fanatical of Hitler's armed forces. As the war progressed the SS became 'a state within a state' with its own business empire composed of armaments and construction companies. Much of these enterprises were run using slave labour from concentration camps.

Himmler was also something of a crank. He was obsessed with the notion of a mystical German past shrouded in paganism. He despatched researchers across Europe and as far as Tibet in the quest for traces of Aryan ancestry. He saw the SS as an order of the Teutonic Knights and he organised strange mystical ceremonies in Wewelsburg Castle. Meetings were held in which his twelve leading men were designated places around a circular Arthurian table surrounded by fake medieval coats of arms.

Although by 1944 the war was going badly, it also marked Himmler's apogee. There were by now more than a million members in the SS and Himmler was to receive more accolades. Following the July Bomb Plot Hitler gave more military responsibility to his most trusted follower. He was assigned control of Army Group Vistula facing the Russian steamroller, but ultimately it was a step too far as his health collapsed under the pressure.

As the end approached he put out peace feelers to the Swedish Red Cross, but Hitler heard of his betrayal and dismissed him. He committed suicide when he was arrested by British military police in May 1945.

74. Ian Fleming Was a Would-be James Bond

Everybody is familiar with the books (and films) of the author Ian Fleming; however, few realise that the wartime experiences of the writer were the inspiration for his novels. His work in naval intelligence led him to become involved in many daring and behind-the-scenes operations.

Fleming had a wealthy family background and went to Eton before making a failed attempt to enter the Foreign Office. Later he tried working as a financier and stockbroker but found he was unsuited to the roles. None of this prepared him for the position he was to assume just prior to the outbreak of war in September 1939. However, he did have a gift for languages and had worked as a journalist, and this may have had a bearing on his first appointment.

He was recruited by Rear Admiral John Godfrey, head of the Naval Intelligence Division, to be his assistant. Godfrey later became his model for 'M'. Fleming was given the code name '17F' and worked in Room 39 in the Admiralty. He immediately showed a talent for administration and writing reports. He was also a fount of ideas. One of these was a proposal to help Bletchley get hold of some enigma code books. He suggested that some British servicemen (dressed in enemy uniforms) should land a German bomber in the sea off the coast of Nazi-occupied France. It was then hoped that a German motor torpedo boat would be lured out to the rescue, which could then be ambushed. The boat and the enigma code book could then be brought back to England. Unfortunately, it was impossible to locate any enemy boats in the area and so the plan was abandoned.

Another idea was floating a corpse off the Continent with some false documents on it. This indeed became reality with Operation Mincemeat (Fact 60). Operation Goldeneye in 1941 was a plan to carry out sabotage and spying missions should the Germans occupy Gibraltar but this never required implementation.

Fleming's greatest contribution was the creation of an elite commando unit called 30 Assault Unit (30 AU). Its remit was to move ahead or behind advancing armies and to 'pinch' any useful document or assault strategic points. Fleming determined the unit's missions and these included Dieppe in 1942 and later Sicily and Italy, where it distinguished itself. Finally, 30 AU took part in D-Day and immediately thereafter.

After D-Day Fleming helped create T-Force (the T is for target). This was a special group whose task was to secure important equipment and documents as Allied forces moved into Germany. Its greatest success was to seize the German V-2 rocket and jet engine research establishment in Kiel. Fleming used the activities of this unit as a basis for many of his books, in particular *Moonraker*.

Fleming never did take part in any of the exciting daredevil schemes he helped draw up. However, the imagination he displayed was later deployed in his now famous works written in the 1950s and '60s.

75. The French Resistance Plays Its Part

After the fall of France in June 1940 open resistance to Nazi occupation was slow to get going. By 1943, however, resistance groups were becoming a thorn in the side of the Germans. This had not come about unassisted. As mentioned before (Fact 65) the SOE in London was very much involved in building up the movement by supplying weapons, trained fighters, and wireless sets etc. By the time of D-Day (the Allied invasion in Normandy) the resistance were providing vital information as well as leaving a trail of havoc.

The situation after the defeat of France was a complex one. To begin with the country itself had become split into two parts. Nazi-occupied France lay in the north and west and Fascist Vichy France was under the control of the dictatorial Marshall Pétain in the south. This somewhat divided the loyalties of the French people as some supported the right-wing marshal.

The resistance also was not one united body. General Charles de Gaulle had first raised the banner of resistance from London in June 1940. He had made his famous 'Appeal of 18 June' exhorting his countrymen to continue the fight, and those who joined de Gaulle became known as the Free French. However, another strong resistance group grew up based in Algeria called the AMF and there were also the communists who the British refused to support.

Hundreds of agents were dropped into France in support of the resistance. The different 'circuits' gave themselves coded names such 'Farmer' or 'Prosper' and London communicated with these groups via Morse code sent on wireless sets. The BBC also sent out pre-agreed nonsense messages over the air waves, which could be the trigger for action; for example, *'Aesculape n'aime pas le mouton'*.

(Aesculape doesn't like mutton). An indication of the success of these groups was the actions of 'Farmer' in 1943 (in north-east France), which claimed to have destroyed forty railway trucks and to be derailing fifteen to twenty trains a week! Meanwhile, 'Prosper' was assassinating at least one German every day in Paris.

On the 'Night of Neptune', the code name for D-Day, the resistance carried out 950 'interruptions' or acts of sabotage on the French railway system alone. Perhaps the most celebrated action was that on the Second SS Panzer Division 'Das Reich', which was resting and refitting near Toulouse in the south of France at the time of the Allied landing. The unit was desperate to get to the beachheads and stop the Allied advance. The quickest method was by train, but the resistance had placed ground carborundum instead of axle oil in the rail transporters. The result was that the wheels soon seized up. Infuriated, the elite forces had to go by road, where they encountered further delays courtesy of the resistance. The SS troops arrived thirteen days late – too late to stop the Allied breakout.

Despite the dangers of daily arrest, torture and execution, the resistance made a massive contribution to Allied success on D-Day.

76. The Allies Leave Nothing to Chance

Allied military leaders realised that only meticulous planning would guarantee success for the planned invasion of France. Attacking well-manned defensive positions had historically been fraught with difficulty and the outcome had often been uncertain – one only has to think of the traditional problem of seizing a castle in medieval times. Added to this the Allies were attacking from across the sea. Failure to break through would mean utter disaster.

The Allies had learnt a great deal from recent events, in particular from the Anglo-Canadian raid on Dieppe in 1942, which had gone badly due to poor planning and insufficient reconnaissance and research beforehand. They were not about to make the same mistake again. To begin with they had an advantage not open to any invading armies previously, which was the information from Bletchley Park regarding the strength and dispositions of nearly all enemy forces in the area of the Normandy beaches. The local French resistance was also helpful in this regard. Aerial surveillance added information about the numerous beach defences and the heavy defensive fortifications and gun emplacements. These were part of Hitler's fortress Europe, which the Allies would have to smash through.

A further Allied concern was the nature of the beaches. They intended to use tanks to help prosecute the advance on the beachheads. However, the wrong kind of sand could leave tanks stranded. As early as December 1943 British submarines had secretly dropped off small units that had taken back sand samples and parts of the beach defences themselves under the very noses of the enemy. The results of tests confirmed the viability of using heavy vehicles in the invasion.

The invading Allied forces would have to deal with heavily mined beaches strewn with various metal obstructions. The British came up with a solution to this problem by placing various attachments onto the fronts of their tanks. These became known as 'Hobart's funnies', named after a certain Major-General Percy Hobart. Examples were the Crab, which was a Sherman tank with a flail of weighted chains for mines, and the AVRE, which was fitted with a large mortar device capable of destroying bunkers. There were many more.

A major preoccupation was how to keep the forces supplied once ashore. Normandy presented a problem as there was no harbour there. The Allies came up with a clever solution, which was to bring two of their own ones with them – they were called Mulberry and were composed of massive steel and concrete structures. They also brought along Pluto an undersea pipeline, which carried oil all the way across the Channel.

The Allies, of course, had two aces up their sleeves: complete control of both the air and the sea. On D-Day itself they would be able to field 10,000 planes against an almost non-existent Luftwaffe. Both this and a myriad of battleships would give the attacking forces overwhelming firepower on the day.

Nevertheless, the Allies would only be sure of success if they could retain one key element: surprise.

77. HITLER EXPECTS VICTORY OVER THE ALLIES

As early as September 1942 Hitler had set out his plans for an Atlantic Wall that would run from the Arctic Circle to the Pyrenees. Despite decreeing that it should be ready in under a year, by the time of the Normandy Landings it was still not completed. Nevertheless, as the summer of that year approached the Führer had felt confident that his 'fortress' was now sufficiently prepared and that he could repel any invasion attempt. His generals, though, were feeling less sanguine.

One reason his generals felt uneasy is that the whole strategy was surely wrong. Hadn't Hitler created his own Maginot Line? It would be difficult to defend the whole length of the wall in equal strength and the Allies could choose when and where to attack with massive force. His generals would have much preferred to hold back their forces and retain some kind of flexibility of response.

On the other hand, the German High Command could point to the quality and strength of the army units available for the defence of northern France. Generalfeldmarschall Gerd von Rundstedt, the Commander-in-Chief West, had as many as 850,000 troops under his control. Some of these represented the best the German Army could field; for example, there were several panzer divisions of the Waffen SS with a total of 16,000 tanks available and some of these included the mighty Tiger tanks, however, several of the infantry divisions were definitely of rather indifferent quality. After years of warfare the high command had had to use men who were either relatively old or very young. In a monument to German efficiency there were 'ear and stomach battalions' in the coastal defence. Bizarrely, these units were made up entirely of those with stomach wounds or who had suffered loss of hearing. Perhaps most surprising were the *Osttruppen*.

These were Russian and Polish recruits who had sworn loyalty to the Nazi regime to save themselves from the death camps. Their reliability was highly suspect.

How to deal with the impending invasion was a problem that vexed the minds of Hitler's generals. Rommel wanted the panzer units close to the beaches so that they could quickly snuff out the enemy forces, while von Rundstedt wanted the tanks held back. In the end Hitler came up with his own solution, which was to keep them in reserve but under his own control.

The timing of the attack remained an enigma. Some German commanders had predicted the landing in May, which indeed was the original month set for it. When this didn't happen there was a general feeling that it might be the end of June or in August. The poor weather at the beginning of June had led them to believe a landing was unlikely at that moment. Or maybe it was all a hoax?

The timing of the landings added an extra element of surprise for the Allies.

78. XX Agent Garbo Is Decorated by Both King George VI and Adolf Hitler

As in all wars throughout history the combatants have tried to secretly infiltrate themselves into the enemy camp and discover exactly what the opposition are planning and thereby steal an advantage. In the Second World War the German secret service, or *Abwehr*, made several attempts to get their agents set up in Britain – all without success!

The Head of German intelligence, Admiral Wilhelm Canaris, was in fact anti-Nazi and secretly plotting against Hitler. This no doubt had some bearing on the sheer ineptitude of German espionage efforts. Spies planted by the Germans in Britain before the war were soon rounded up as they were well known to the authorities. Further attempts made in the early years to infiltrate were also easily dealt with. For example, typically, would-be spies were dropped off by submarine or by boat in some quiet coastal area. They would immediately arouse suspicion due to their wet clothing, the large amount of money they were carrying and incorrect documentation. All those captured were offered a choice by Britain's own secret service, MI5. They could either become double agents working for the British or face execution. Some agreed to work for MI5, and this was the beginning of the double-cross network that was to have profound consequences.

Once German spies had been 'turned' they would be given the messages they were to transmit back to their handlers in Berlin. A story was usually built up of how the German spy had managed to get work and the information he had allegedly 'picked up' was fed to the credulous *Abwehr*.

There were also other double-cross spies who were nationals of third countries who managed to convince the German authorities of their desire to spy for Germany while in fact working for the Allies. Three of these were Dusko Popov (code-named Tricycle), a Polish officer named Brutus and a Spaniard called Garbo. All three had an important part to play in the deception plans leading up to D-Day.

Garbo's real name was Juan Pujol Garcia. At first he operated by himself from Lisbon before moving to the UK. He built up a collection of twenty-seven fictional sub-agents who were supposedly supplying him with important snippets of information. The Gestapo believed him and paid out vast sums of money as gratitude for his help. When it came to D-Day Garbo and his 'agents' had plenty of disinformation to relay, particularly in relation to FUSAG, an imaginary army lined up in Kent for a supposed attack on Calais. Garbo did eventually tell the Germans the truth about the Normandy Landings, but only when it was too late. Hitler was so impressed with his copious detailed messages about Allied armies that he awarded him (over the radio) the Iron Cross Second Class in July 1944. Later the same year King George VI awarded him an MBE as well. Not many spies in the Second World War could boast of being so handsomely rewarded.

79. The Führer Is Led on a Wild Goose Chase

One of the most fascinating elements of the story leading up to D-Day is the web of misinformation fed to the Germans by the Allies. As Hitler increasingly took all the key military decisions these deceptions were targeted specifically at the German leader. While he remained isolated in his mountain retreat of Berchtesgaden or in his 'Wolf's Lair' in East Prussia he increasingly became the dupe of the Allies.

The aim of the deceptions was to get Hitler to divert his forces away from Normandy and to spread them around his empire. The code name for this was 'Bodyguard' after a comment by Churchill that truth was so precious that it should be surrounded by 'a bodyguard of lies'. One part of this deception plan was called 'Zeppelin'. This was an operation designed to convince the Germans that an Anglo-American attack was imminent on Yugoslavia and Greece designed to link up with the advancing Soviet armies. This was a vulnerable area for Germany as Bulgaria and Rumania were trying to wriggle out of the Axis alliance – the latter was a key supplier of oil for the *Wehrmacht*. Hitler became convinced after a pro-German Turkish spy code named 'Cicero' brought photographs of top-secret documents from the British embassy in Ankara. They were in fact a plant. However, Hitler fell for the stunt and moved twenty-five divisions that could have been available on D-Day into the Balkans.

Meanwhile Operation Fortitude was a two-pronged deception. Fortitude North focused on trying to convince the German warlord that an attack on Norway was being planned. The airwaves became filled with false messages sent out from radio operators in Edinburgh and elsewhere in Scotland. Supposedly, an impending attack was being prepared by two non-existent Allied armies. The Germans consulted their 'reliable' agents Tricycle and Garbo (Fact 78), who confirmed the increase of military activity north of the border. Again Hitler became convinced of the threat and decided to station nearly half a million troops in Norway. Von Rundstedt contemptuously observed that by trying to hold on to everything Hitler would eventually lose everything.

Fortitude South, on the other hand, was designed to get the Germans to believe that the D-Day attack would come against Calais. A fictitious Allied army group called FUSAG was built up in Kent, headed by the eminent American general George S. Patton. Again the Germans were bombarded by increased radio traffic. Luftwaffe flights were allowed over the area so that they could photograph real-looking inflatable Sherman tanks and landing craft made of plywood and canvass. Hitler was persuaded and kept his massive 15th Army in readiness behind Calais. Incredibly, even after D-Day the Nazi leader kept to the view that the real attack was still to come and that the Normandy landings were merely a diversion.

It is remarkable that Hitler was so easily persuaded by Allied subterfuge, especially as he had fallen for similar tricks previously. However, the fact that these ruses were consistently confirmed by double agents made them all the more credible for the beleaguered dictator.

80. Japanese Forces are Defeated on the Tennis Court

After the epic withdrawal of British forces from Burma in 1942, the following year saw a kind of standoff. The Japanese completed the Burmese railway line, which would permit them to bring up more forces while the Allies were slowing rebuilding their armies after endless defeats. However, by the beginning of 1944 both sides felt able to launch their own offensives: the British to throw the Japanese out of Burma and the Japanese to invade India.

The Commonwealth armies under General 'Bill' Slim had been reinvigorated and given a new strategy for taking on the enemy. Instead of retreating if surrounded, Allied troops were expected to hold a 'defensive box' and await supply drops from the air and a relieving army. The aim was to defeat the Japanese at their own game – jungle warfare.

The Japanese brought forward 100,000 men for their massive offensive called U-GO. By March the offensive got going with the objective of taking Imphal and Kohima, which were strategic points on the gateway to India. Already by the end of March the road between the two had been cut and at Kohima the picture soon became grim. Kohima was in fact a village perched at 5,000 feet above sea level and with only a garrison of 1,000 British and Commonwealth forces. An epic battle now followed. From 4 April for a period of ten days the Japanese launched ferocious infantry and artillery assaults that left the tiny garrison in a perilous state; it has been described as 'fighting as desperate as any in recorded history'. In the end the garrison, lacking water and suffering heavy casualties, was reduced to defending an area on one side of a tennis court. However, just in time a relieving Indian army arrived, but it took a further two months before the Japanese retreated.

At the same time Imphal was also besieged with a similar scenario. The Japanese continually mounted determined attacks with almost suicidal intensity, resulting in heavy casualties but with no breakthrough. Towards the end of May the enemy made a final desperate assault from west and south on Imphal, which, however, was repulsed. In total the siege had lasted eighty-eight days with both sides being taken to the limits of endurance. But by 4 July the Japanese commanders ceased the U-GO offensive due to starvation of their troops and a one in two casualty rate. In total Japanese losses amounted to 55,000 men against 12,063 Commonwealth soldiers.

This story would not be complete, however, without including the participation of the Chindits. These were a British 'Special Force' created by a maverick commander called Orde Wingate, whose task was guerrilla warfare deep behind enemy lines. Suffering terrible jungle privations, they performed acts of sabotage such as cutting important railway links and attacking enemy positions. This forced the Japanese to divert sizeable forces away from their offensive.

By April 1944 Commonwealth forces had swept the Japanese out of Burma. This victory is one of the forgotten stories of the war, with General Slim very much the unsung hero.

81. The D-Day Landings Go Better than Expected

By the spring of 1944 southern England was already heaving with personnel and vehicles in preparation for the greatest seaborne invasion in history. Apart from the Americans and the British themselves, there were troops from various countries including Canada, France and Poland. Out at sea 138 battleships and as many as 7,000 other vessels, including landing craft, were being mustered. In addition, 10,000 aircraft were being readied for action. In total 6 million personnel would be involved in the whole massive operation.

Heading the whole Allied expedition was the American General Dwight D. Eisenhower. He was the leader of SHAEF (Supreme Allied Headquarters of the Allied Expeditionary Force) and had been selected for the role as he had shown himself adept at soothing inter-Allied tensions. The British and Canadians would land on the Eastern three invasion beaches – Juno for the Canadians, Sword and Gold for the British. The Americans would seize the Utah and Gold beachheads to the west. There were also to be commando parachute drops and glider landings behind German lines in order to secure strategic points and to impede counter-attacks.

Quite by accident the weather provided the Allies with the perfect cover. The landings had been fixed for 5 June as the tides were right at that moment. The Allied troops embarked ready for action only to find out that stormy conditions made a cross-Channel attack impracticable. However, a sudden lull allowed the Allies to still go ahead but with one-day delay. The unexpected improvement in the weather meant surprise was total.

As dawn approached on 6 June the German defenders could see the Allied armada emerge out of the mist on the far horizon. Immediately a huge naval bombardment was unleashed on the enemy defences as a prelude to the landings. Waves of bombers were also sent in. Specially designed landing craft called LCVPs then ferried the troops to the beaches.

The British and Canadians met relatively light resistance and were able to advance inland by as much as 25 miles by the end of the day. On Omaha beach the Americans were presented with the task of scaling a 100-foot escarpment using rockets that fired grappling hooks and attached ropes. Unfortunately, the cliffs also presented the Germans with an excellent defensive position. Bad luck and confusion meant that by the end of the day they had only secured a small strip of land and at the cost of 2,000 men. Utah Beach on the other hand represented the big success story of the day. A major breakthrough meant that within fifteen hours there were as many as 20,000 troops ashore.

Meanwhile, back at Von Rundstedt's headquarters all was not well. He desperately wanted to release the panzer forces, unleash them at the beachheads and send the Allies back into the sea. Unfortunately, the Führer slept till noon and only by 4 p.m. was permission granted. But it was all too late and the opportunity had passed. Nothing now could stop the relentless Allied build-up of men and materiel.

82. British Troops Enjoyed a Nice Cup of Tea on the Normandy Beaches!

The various national armies certainly had their different characteristics as fighting forces. You might say the Japanese were the most ferocious and fearless. In Europe the Germans were certainly the most professional while the Italians had the reputation for being the least so. This was undoubtedly due to the Italian troops being poorly led and motivated as well as lacking sufficient military hardware. Russian troops, however, fought determinedly for their homeland. The British and American armies provided a striking contrast.

Like the British, the American soldiers were civilian conscripts. To begin with the GIs were green and unprepared for battlefield situations, but they were adaptable and quick to learn. American generals were also quite cavalier about pushing their men forward irrespective of losses in order to achieve a victory. However, like all Western democracies they had a reliance on heavy bombing and artillery bombardments to avoid unnecessary casualties. This inevitably resulted in many civilian losses as happened in Normandy.

The British on the other hand were certainly more cautious than their counterparts. They had been in the war for far longer than the Americans and were experiencing manpower shortages. There was also a fear of failure due to previous reverses at Dunkirk and elsewhere. Perhaps this is why British troops were clearly much better in defence than in attack, as was noted by the Germans themselves.

The British Army also had its own rather bizarre idiosyncrasies. There was, you might say, a kind of trade-union mentality. To begin with, there was an attitude whereby you were expected to keep rigidly to your job;

for example, a sapper would not join in the fighting once his particular engineering task had been completed. Likewise, an infantryman would reluctantly help to get a lorry out of difficulties if it was part of his unit.

A further amazing fact is that British troops had regular tea breaks even in the heat of battle on D-Day. It was noted by Canadian observers that hardly had they waded ashore when some of them felt the desperate need to have a quick brew and a smoke even though the beaches were still under fire. The Americans were particularly incensed that on D-Day the British failed to immediately pursue the Germans beyond the beachheads but preferred to settle back for a well-earned cuppa. One Canadian trooper typically joked that the British couldn't fight for 'three and a half minutes without tea'.

A final point about the differences between the armies fighting in Europe is that many German units really did believe in fighting to the last man. Most were indoctrinated into thinking that they were fighting for their country's survival whereas the Allied soldiers were more intent on surviving and getting it over with. Most Allied soldiers, then, did not really believe in holding out in impossible situations and were more likely to surrender after having put up a decent struggle.

This is not to denigrate the amazing courage of those who came ashore on D-Day and who risked their lives to liberate Europe.

83. Hitler Unleashes His Secret Weapons

By 1942 the war had started to go badly for the Nazi regime. The Soviet Union had not collapsed as expected and Germany was facing a long and protracted war on the Eastern front. The British, too, had refused to negotiate and it would only be a matter of time before the Allies teamed up to create a second front. It was now that Hitler gave the go-ahead for research and production of secret weapons, which he hoped could alter the course of the war. Experts in London had begun to hear reports of these weapons, which were being test fired from an isolated coastal area in north-east Germany called Peenemünde. But what was going on there exactly?

From aerial observations the Allies could ascertain that some kind of rocketry was being produced there. The V-1 was in fact a kind of flying bomb with a powerful explosive mix of TNT and ammonium nitrate in the warhead. The V-2 on the other hand was a fearsome rocket with a 1-ton high-explosive payload that could fly to 100,000 feet at 3,600 mph before falling back to earth. Hitler hoped that these devastating weapons, if produced in sufficient quantities, could literally knock Britain out of the war. In August 1943 the British, realising the threat, bombed the site and thereby delayed production but did not destroy the project. As a result of this, however, the Germans moved the site underground inside a mountain in central Germany. They were now able to set about mass-producing their dastardly weapons.

Once the Allies had established themselves on the D-Day beaches Hitler immediately ordered that his V-1s be fired on London. These weapons required special ramps to be set up in order to fire them off. Several of these were now lined up on the northern coast of France facing the British capital. They struck terror into Londoners as their flight was accompanied by a sinister monotonous drone. Once they had reached their target the engines would cut out, signifying immediate danger for all those below. Around 13,000 V-1s were launched against Britain. However, many missed their targets and British pilots developed a technique of flying alongside the V-1s and 'tipping their wings' over which immediately sent them spiralling to the ground.

The V-2s were more devastating and even more frightening. However, the first ones were not ready until September 1944. The rockets did not require ramps but could be launched vertically from any chosen site. They would land without warning and their explosive power could demolish a whole street. Hitler had hoped to fire a relentless stream of these rockets onto London from a special massive bunker facility near Calais. Heavy Allied bombing put paid to it, but Hitler's dream lived on. In the end only 1,359 rockets reached London. In total almost 9,000 British lives were lost to the V-1s and V-2s.

As with all the Nazi miracle weapons, their arrival on the scene could be summed up as 'too little, too late'.

84. A Tale of Two Prima Donnas

The Allies may have successfully consolidated the areas surrounding the initial landing sites but breaking out from here was not so easy. The Germans had clearly lost the immediate opportunity to destroy the enemy but the Führer's order was not to give an inch. This did deny his army flexibility, but for some weeks the invading armies remained bottled up as a result.

By 7 July the Allied forces in Normandy already numbered a million and with the massive build-up of tanks and other materiel it was only a matter of time before a breakthrough came about. In addition, the Germans were severely hampered by enemy control of the skies.

In some ways the period of the weeks after D-Day is the story of two prima donnas. One of these was General Bernard Montgomery (Monty), who was temporarily in control of all Allied ground forces. He has been described as breathtakingly conceited, opinionated, and egotistical. It is little wonder, then, that the Americans found him difficult to get along with. He had hoped to take Caen (a large French city nearby) within the first day after the landing, but fierce enemy resistance made this impossible. The Germans had placed their best tank forces in and around the city and, after several attempts, he had made little progress. On 7 July the city had been heavily bombed and on 17 July he decided to destroy German positions around the city in a 2,600-bomber raid (pity the poor French!) prior to a huge offensive called Operation Goodwood. This attack had mixed results for although Caen was at last taken, the Germans had been able to knock out nearly 200 British tanks, which the Germans contemptuously called 'Tommy brewers'. Monty, as always, called it a great success, but the Americans thought otherwise.

The other prima donna was the American General George Patton. His speeches to his troops were often blunt and peppered with profanities – hence the reason he was known as 'Old Blood and Guts'. Strangely, he believed he might have been a reincarnated general from Roman times or the Napoleonic Wars. Unlike Montgomery, who planned meticulously and was often cautious, Patton believed in bold, swift advances and leading from the front.

Monty claimed his flawed offensive was all part of a master plan to draw German forces towards Caen and away from the American western sector. Until now they, too, had made little progress due to a feature of the French countryside here called the *bocage* (small fields with dense raised hedges), which the Germans defended well. On 25 July, however, the Americans exploited the new opportunity by launching their own offensive preceded by more carpet bombing. The German front, already overstretched, soon collapsed and they raced through to Avranches on the west coast. Leading the charge was Patton. After a brief diversion into Brittany his forces swept eastwards linking up with the British and Canadians at Falaise and thereby trapping over 50,000 German troops.

The way to Paris was now open and on 25 August it was duly liberated.

85. Hitler Has a Hair-raising Experience

With the war obviously lost some of Hitler's own generals had decided that the time had come to rid themselves of this incompetent corporal. It would only be a matter of time before the Allied armies from the West and Soviet armies from the East entered the Reich itself. The hope was that a deal could be cut with the Allies if Hitler was removed.

The main problem for any plotters was getting close to the dictator as he was extremely well guarded. However, a certain Colonel Count Claus von Stauffenberg came up with a seemingly fail-safe plan. He had a remarkable appearance as due to the war he had lost an eye, his right hand and two fingers on his left. He was in an ideal situation as he had managed to become Chief of Staff of the Replacement Army in Berlin and regularly attended meetings at Hitler's headquarters in the 'Wolf's Lair' in east Prussia. The plan (Operation Valkyrie) required Stauffenberg to place a briefcase containing a bomb next to Hitler, then return to Berlin where his fellow conspirators would organise the arrest of the Nazi leadership and set up a provisional government.

On the appointed day, 20 July 1944, he arrived at Hitler's headquarters for a conference, set the fuse on the bomb in the bathroom and placed the briefcase by a table leg near the Führer. He later left the room on the pretext of making a phone call. Minutes later there was a massive explosion. Stauffenberg was convinced Hitler could not have survived, so he phoned through to his accomplices in Berlin to activate the plan and headed out of the compound.

Hitler had survived, however. He was fortunate indeed that the conference had not been held in the normal concrete bunker but in a wooden building above ground. This meant the power of the blast was dispersed through the windows and thin walls. In addition, the briefcase had, by chance, been moved to the other side of a table leg distancing him from the explosion. Four military personnel died but the Führer staggered out alive with only minor injuries. One of his secretaries noted that he had an almost comical appearance with his hair standing on end and his trousers shredded. Hitler put his survival down to providence and demanded revenge.

The dictator later made contact with Goebbels, the Propaganda Minister, who had his offices in Berlin. With the minister was Major Otto Remer of the Berlin Guards Battalion. Remer was a fanatical Nazi who had been informed that Hitler was dead and was reluctantly following the plotter's orders. Hitler bellowed down the phone to Remer, 'Do you recognise my voice? This is Adolf Hitler.' Immediately Remer now set about arresting the plotters themselves. Some of the coup leaders, including Stauffenberg, were unceremoniously marched out into a courtyard and shot. Others later on had a slow grizzly death by hanging on meathooks. In total around 5,000 arrests were made.

Ironically, this assassination attempt strengthened Hitler's position and his determination to continue the war.

86. French Pilots Fly for the USSR

One of the more remarkable stories of the Second World War is that of a French fighter squadron which was sent to fight for the Soviet Union. It was the brainchild of Free French leader Charles de Gaulle, who wanted French servicemen to be involved on all fronts in the war.

In the early years of the war the Soviet Union was in dire straits and only too pleased to receive any assistance. De Gaulle dubbed his squadron the Normandie and they were duly despatched in September 1942. The twelve pilots and forty-seven ground crew travelled by rail and air via Iran and Azerbaijan to their airbase inside Russia. Training was carried out in temperatures of -25 to -30 degrees Celsius, but by March 1943 the unit was operational. They were soon in the thick of the fighting and acquitted themselves well. Although they received reinforcements which made up three more squadrons, they tragically suffered losses of twenty-one pilots within the first six months.

In 1944 Soviet leader Stalin was so pleased with their performance that he added Niemen to their title in memory of the river they had helped to liberate.

At the war's end the Normandie-Niemen claimed to have downed 273 enemy planes as well as destroying numerous trains and vehicles. Of the nearly 100 pilots who participated forty-two did not return. They received many medals from both France and the Soviet Union and these included the *Legion of Honour*, the *Order of Lenin* and *Heroes of the Soviet Union*.

They were most certainly heroes!

87. American Island-Hopping Keeps the Japanese on the Hop

By the end of 1942 the Americans had achieved significant naval victories over the Japanese, but the war was far from over. The most direct route to the Japanese homeland lay in attacking across the Pacific where the enemy were firmly entrenched on countless islands. Taking every heavily fortified island fortress could be costly and time-consuming, so in 1943 the USA came up with a cunning policy of 'island-hopping', which meant seizing strategically important islands and bypassing those that were deemed of little significance. In their relentless advance towards Japan they kept the enemy guessing when and where the next assault would come.

By October 1944 'island-hopping' was in full swing. Although the Americans were able to deploy overwhelming numbers of men, planes and ships, this did not guarantee them any easy victories. With the deteriorating situation the Japanese became evermore desperate in defence of their positions; for example, in the naval Battle of Leyte, off the Philippines, they threw in everything including, for the first time, kamikaze fighter planes. Leyte has gone down as the largest naval battle in history and left the Japanese fleet seriously depleted. The American fleet was virtually unscathed but the battle to control the Philippines continued unabated as enemy ground troops fought with suicidal fanaticism. In November, the Americans attacked Luzon in the north of the Philippines when the enemy also fielded kaiten, which were suicide torpedo craft. The battle for the Philippines raged on until mid-1945 and resulted in the loss of around 200,000 Japanese and 10,000 American lives.

Meanwhile, the tiny island of Iwo Jima was already in Uncle Sam's sights. Since the end of 1944 American bombers had been making 3,000-mile round trips to Japan from the Mariana Islands. If they could seize the island they would be only 760 miles away, allowing the bombers fighter escorts. The battle there raged for a whole month between February and March 1945, leaving 20,000 Japanese dead. Such was the ferocity of the conflict that only 212 men or 1 per cent of the garrison surrendered. The engagement is remembered in history by the iconic photograph of American marines raising the stars and stripes over Mount Suribachi (although it was, in fact, the second one raised there that day!).

Okinawa was just 350 miles from the southern Japanese island of Kyushu and its capture would mark the final stage before invasion. In April the Americans fielded half a million men and 1,300 ships for the epic engagement. The Japanese defended with 120,000 men and 10,000 planes (many of these were kamikaze) and a new desperate weapon dubbed the *baka*. This was a rocket-powered glider whose nose was charged with 1 ton of explosive and was guided to its target by a lone pilot. Although several American ships succumbed to these desperado tactics, the result was not in doubt and of the Japanese defenders a mere 7,000 survived.

The American leadership now pondered the likely cost of invading mainland Japan.

88. Arnhem Was a Bridge Too Far

After the liberation of Paris in August the Allies had made rapid progress across France and within a month they were on the borders of Hitler's Germany. The mood in the Allied camp was one of euphoria and many believed that the war would be over by Christmas. Front line officers, however, noted that German resistance was stiffening as they approached the Reich.

General Dwight D. Eisenhower (Ike), the Supreme Commander of Allied forces, had insisted that all the armies under his control would advance on a broad front across France. However, the British General Montgomery (Monty) was contemptuous of this approach. In forthright fashion he told the American that the war could be finished quickly if he, Monty, could be allowed to cross into Germany alone and push his armies all the way to Berlin. Inexplicably, Ike agreed.

The operation was named Market Garden and was set for 17 September. From its inception it was badly planned and the British general seemed to cast aside all the caution for which he was famed. The scheme envisaged mainly British forces seizing the bridge at Arnhem in Holland and thereby avoiding having to directly attack across the Rhine. The Allied armies were still 65 miles south of Arnhem, so American airborne forces would be required to seize bridges at Eindhoven, Grave and Nijmegen allowing the British XXX Corps to make a speedy dash up the narrow road. Their task was to reach Arnhem within forty-eight hours and link up with the Ist British Airborne Division, which, in the meantime, would be dropped in the vicinity of the bridge and would hold it until the Corps' arrival. The astute reader will immediately be aware that the whole plan was fraught with risk.

Monty exuded optimism about the operation despite warnings that there were definite sightings of an SS Panzer Division refitting near Arnhem. On the morning of 17 September elements of the British airborne unit landed by glider 8 miles from Arnhem. Immediately, they encountered fierce German resistance but were unable to report back as all the radios failed to function. However, by dusk one battalion of paratroopers was holding the north end of the bridge but could advance no further. It all now depended on XXX Corps.

Alas, this relief unit was making disappointingly slow progress due to ferocious German defence of the canal and river crossings. A further problem was that the corps was unable to operate off the narrow road due to the streams and dykes on either side. However, by the evening of 20 September Nijmegen was cleared. They were now only 10 miles from Arnhem. But it was all too late. The next morning the single battalion holding the bridge was overwhelmed by two SS Panzer divisions. A few days later, in the dead of night, 2,500 paratroopers managed to slip south over the River Nederrijin, but 3,800 fell into German hands.

Monty immediately claimed 90 per cent success but it was clearly a failure. He had had his chance and blown it. The 'broad front' strategy was reinstated.

89. THE WARSAW UPRISING IS ANOTHER POLISH TRAGEDY

The story of the Polish people in the Second World War is one of endless and terrible suffering. From the very beginning of the war their country had been divided up and occupied by two of the nastiest dictatorships of the twentieth century – Nazi Germany and the Soviet Union. Hitler's creed was that Slavic people were an inferior race and so the Poles were subjected to a regime of heinous brutality. Polish Jews were forced to live in a ghetto in Warsaw and a rising there in 1943 was crushed ruthlessly by the SS. By the autumn of 1944, however, the Germans were in full retreat and the Polish people at last saw a chance to liberate themselves.

For the Russians 1944 had turned into something of an *annus mirabilis*. Stalin had launched Operation Bagration in June and it had resulted in the virtual destruction of Hitler's Army Group Centre with nearly a million men killed, wounded or captured. Such a hole had been punched in the German front line that the way was now clear for Soviet armies to enter parts of Germany itself in the north and Poland in the centre. By the end of July Russian forces were already approaching the River Vistula, which bordered Poland.

It was at this very moment that the Polish resistance in Warsaw decided to rise up against Nazi occupation. Timing was crucial as the Soviet dictator had his own government, composed of Polish communists, ready and waiting to be installed in the capital. Those in Warsaw saw a chance to set up their own provisional government prior to the Soviet arrival. Many Polish soldiers and airmen had fought alongside Britain in the hope that the Allies would help in establishing such an outcome.

On 1 August 1944 the Polish Home Army began their revolt. It was expected that the Germans would soon abandon Warsaw, especially as Soviet armies were a short distance away. However, they soon showed their intent on mercilessly crushing the uprising. Meanwhile, Soviet forces watched and did nothing to help the beleaguered Poles.

The Home Army fought valiantly but they were ill-equipped with only 14 per cent of them armed. They were facing the might of elite Waffen SS troops as well as Stuka dive bombers and tanks. At one point 1,500 defenders were trapped in the old town but managed to escape down manholes into the city sewers. Amazingly the resistance held out for sixty-three days but the end was never in doubt. Around 15,000 Poles died in the battle with a similar number of Germans killed. Himmler's revenge was to send 154,000 Polish men women and children to concentration camps before razing the city to the ground.

The Soviets always claimed that their troops needed resting and their supply and communications systems were overstretched. Whatever the truth of the situation, it suited Stalin to see the Polish Home Army eradicated. When the Russian steamroller moved forward in January 1945 a communist system was quickly established.

90. A Bulge Suddenly Appears ... then Equally Rapidly Disappears

The dear reader should be forgiven for thinking that I inexplicably want to write about an excellent new dieting plan I have discovered. However, the so-called Battle of the Bulge does not relate to any excessive intake of calories but rather to Hitler's ill-advised scheme to inflict a massive defeat on the Allies in the West who were now lined up on the German frontier. The plan was to attack through the Ardennes forest (just as in 1940) and to drive a wedge between the British in the north and the Americans to the south. The objective was the Belgian port of Antwerp, which brought in vital supplies for the Allied armies.

The dictator's own generals advised against it as if it failed there would be fewer forces to take on the fearsome Soviet forces in the east. There were two other problems. Although Hitler could still muster an impressive number of men and tanks, the Allies still controlled the air, making movement during the day impossible. In addition, the Reich was rapidly running out of fuel, meaning that German tanks would be reliant on seizing Allied supply dumps.

Preparations for the offensive went well. Tanks and men were moved around at night and there was complete radio silence during the build-up. Indeed, the Allies had no inkling that an attack was imminent, the assumption being that the German Army was a spent force. When the offensive came, then, surprise was total.

On 16 December 1944 200,000 men and 1,400 tanks poured forth into Allied positions. At first all went well. The weather was ideal as the ground was shrouded in fog, thereby nullifying Allied air activity. Those troops facing the initial onslaught were American units that were either resting up after heavy fighting or were completely green.

Thirty-two English-speaking German soldiers dressed in American uniforms also caused some initial confusion. Although the US 106th and 28th Divisions were decimated (with 8,000 of the former taken prisoner), other units to the north and south held their positions, creating a bulge shape on the map.

Allied forces did not collapse as Hitler had expected. In one famous incident 18,000 Americans were surrounded at Bastogne and when asked to surrender, their commander, Brigadier-General A. J. McAuliffe, replied 'Nuts!'

To the north of the pocket British general Montgomery acted decisively to block the German advance. In the south General Patton turned his armies round 90 degrees to hit the Germans in the flank. After four days the skies cleared, allowing Allied planes to strike German Panzer forces, which in any case had failed to reach their objectives and had run out fuel. Bastogne was relieved by Patton's forces on Boxing Day and by 9 January the offensive had lost all its momentum. By 16 January the British and American armies linked up and soon after the bulge had disappeared completely.

German casualties were nearly 100,000 while the Allies suffered 81,000 with 700 tanks lost on both sides. The enemy could not recover from these huge losses and Hitler had hastened his own demise.

91. President Roosevelt Attends His Final Conference

Franklin D. Roosevelt was America's longest-serving president. He was elected for four terms from 1933 to 1945, which was some achievement given that he had been crippled by polio and was confined to a wheelchair for much of the time. Roosevelt was a charming and charismatic figure and despite his limited success in dealing with the Depression in the 1930s he remained massively popular with many ordinary Americans. When the war came he transformed America into a huge military machine that fought enemies on two fronts: Europe and the Far East.

At various intervals during the war it became necessary for all three of the Allied leaders – Churchill, Roosevelt and the Soviet leader, Josef Stalin – to meet together to discuss overall strategy. From the very beginning of the conflict the American leader had, of course, already developed a close working relationship with his British counterpart. This is hardly surprising as both Churchill and Roosevelt shared a common language (mostly!) and both were leaders of Western democracies. They also enjoyed each other's company and would indulge in dinner parties at the White House, which involved smoking and drinking together late into the night. They were apparently the best of friends. Stalin, however, was a very different proposition. As we have seen he was a secretive and paranoid leader of a brutal communist regime and so working with him might be rather difficult.

The first meeting of the Big Three had taken place in Tehran, the Iranian capital, at the end of 1943. To Churchill's surprise and disappointment Roosevelt had gone out of his way to charm the Soviet leader, calling him 'Uncle Joe', and even made jokes at the British leader's expense. Churchill was forced to ditch his Mediterranean strategy in favour of a direct cross-Channel invasion provisionally set for 1 May 1944. This pleased Stalin, who had been pressing for a second front for some time.

By the time of the next conference of Yalta (February 1945) in the Crimea the American President was clearly a sick man. Pale and gaunt, he was nevertheless prepared to fly halfway round the world to keep the wartime alliance together. Again Churchill was somewhat side-lined. Roosevelt was delighted that Stalin accepted his United Nations project and all sides agreed that Germany would be divided up temporarily between the Big Three and France. A contentious point was Poland, which had recently been overrun by Soviet forces. Rather than being confrontational Roosevelt accepted the 'concession' from the Soviet leader that free and fair elections would be held there. Both Western leaders expressed confidence that Stalin would keep to his promises. It soon became evident that he would not, but there was little that the Western powers could do with millions of Soviet forces occupying Eastern Europe.

Roosevelt died on 12 April 1945. He had been a great president but had shown himself strangely naïve when dealing with the wily Russian leader. Churchill felt the American leader had betrayed their friendship and later failed to attend his funeral.

92. Crossing the Rhine Is a Mighty Operation

After Hitler's failed Ardennes offensive German forces in the West were depleted but still represented a powerful force. In order to break through into Germany proper the Allies still faced a challenging task. First of all they had to overcome the Siegfried Line that lay west of the River Rhine, after which they had to cross the great river itself. It was not going to be easy as the enemy were expected to fight ferociously to defend their homeland.

It was decided to take on the defenders German opposite the northern sector, which lay mainly under Montgomery's control. The Siegfried Line was composed of tank traps, ditches and concrete emplacements but did not offer an insuperable obstruction. Operation Veritable was a two-pronged attack with the British beginning their assault from the north and the Americans from the south. The campaign opened on 5 February 1945 with a 1,000-piece artillery bombardment that lasted for five hours and represented the largest artillery barrage of the Second World War. The next day 200,000 British and Canadians moved forward and, as expected, met stubborn resistance, ultimately causing the loss of 15,000 lives. However, by 5 March they had linked up with the Americans.

The main thrust of the Allied campaign continued in the northern sector opposite the Ruhr, which was Germany's main industrial area. Again Montgomery was given American forces in order to help him force a crossing of the Rhine. The British general set about planning everything meticulously.

Ironically, it was the Americans in the south who made a breakthrough first. Famously, the bridge at Remagen was seized intact on 7 March and elsewhere Patton was itching to lead his armies into the Reich. However, Eisenhower insisted they wait until Monty was ready in keeping with the 'broad front' strategy.

Operation 'Plunder', the code name for the crossing of the Rhine, would be second only to Normandy in its size and complexity. In total 250,000 British and American troops were massed along a 30-kilometre front and Churchill flew over to be there for such a momentous event. On the night of 23 March hostilities began with a massive barrage. In the initial attack men were then ferried across the Rhine on 'buffaloes', which were armoured amphibious troop carriers, while others moved across on special floating DD tanks.

This was followed in the morning by the largest single airborne assault in history. As on D-Day paratroopers and gliders were deployed behind German lines and some 16,000 men were involved. Three columns of planes and gliders, each around 150 miles in length, took two hours to pass and undoubtedly had a demoralising impact on already hard-pressed enemy troops.

Within four days Montgomery had thrown bridges across the river and was able to move in his armoured divisions. Now all along the Rhine Allied forces were crossing the great river and breaking through. The British general headed off north while the Americans soon enveloped a huge army of 300,000 German soldiers in the Ruhr.

It was the beginning of the end.

93. STALIN ORGANISES A RACE

The Soviet leader had been surprised by the rapid advance of the British and Americans in the West. He had anticipated much slower progress giving him plenty of time to take the German capital. He distrusted his erstwhile allies and feared that they would seize Berlin before him and negotiate a separate surrender with the Germans. However, this was far from being in the mind of Eisenhower, who was intent on keeping to the agreed lines of occupation and was expecting to meet Soviet forces halfway across Germany. There seemed to be no sense in losing Allied lives for a city that was clearly in the Soviet zone.

Russian forces were still some way from Berlin but in early April Stalin met with his two top commanders – Marshals G. K. Zhukov and I. S. Konev – and ordered them to go headlong for the German capital. He intimated that it was a competition between them to see who could reach the centre first. The Soviets had overwhelming force and between them the two generals controlled 1.5 million men with massive quantities of tanks and artillery.

The task, however, was by no means easy. Berlin was a huge metropolis and 1 million Germans had been drafted in to hold it. Apart from the elite Waffen SS there were the Hitler Youth and the *Volkssturm* (Home Guard) who were determined to defend the capital to the last man. Zhukov, coming in from the west, was in command of the 1st Belorussian Army Front. At over 900,000 men it represented the mightiest concentration of ground forces ever assembled by the Soviets. Meanwhile, Konev's smaller Ist Ukrainian Army Front was advancing from the south-west.

Zhukov launched his initial attack on the well-defended Seelow Heights outside the capital on 16 April. Massive searchlights were used to accompany first an infantry and then a tank attack. However, German forces put up tremendous resistance and Zhukov's men and armour became enmeshed in a confined space with little progress made. It was only after four days that his forces made it into the outskirts of Berlin. The Soviet Army hero had lost his touch. Meanwhile in the south Konev made more rapid progress through the defensive lines and into the city suburbs.

Fighting in the city streets proved costly for the Soviets. Hitler Youth and *Volksturm* soldiers used the anti-tank *Panzerfaust* with devastating effect on Soviet armour. However, Zhukov, under pressure from Stalin, now sent forward smaller assault groups led by Chuikov (the hero of Stalingrad) to work their way to the centre. On the morning of 25 April forward units of Konev's army arrived at the Tiergarten and found, to their surprise, they were firing on fellow Russians. It was Chuikov's 8th Guards Army who had won the race for Zhukov after all.

On 30 April the Soviet flag was hoisted over the Reichstag, the symbolic heart of the capital. On the same day Hitler committed suicide in his bunker. The formal surrender of the Reich was just days away.

94. Mussolini and His Mistress Are Highly Strung

After his dramatic rescue by Skorzeny in September 1943 (Fact 62) Mussolini was reinstated as fascist dictator. However, his new Republic of Salò was very much a pale imitation of his former glorious empire. For one thing he had very little jurisdiction over his new kingdom, which initially stretched down to south of Rome, as it was all very much under German military control and Mussolini was their puppet. He was even totally dependent on the Germans for financial support. He set himself up in Gargagno on Lake Garda and awaited events.

It was clear from the start that the Italian dictator's regime would only last as long as the Germans could defend it. How long that might be was unclear as Field Marshall Kesselring was putting up a masterly defence of the peninsula by creating strong defensive lines across it. After the fall of Rome in June 1944 German forces fell back to the formidable Gothic Line that went right the way across Italy from Pisa to Rimini and ran just north of Florence. The Germans were also in a favourable position as the Allies had moved some divisions to France, which left Italy as something of a sideshow for General Harold Alexander, the commander in charge of Allied forces there.

The Allies launched an offensive in the autumn of 1944 and breached the line but failed to make much headway due to appalling autumn conditions, thereby making progress across the rivers and mountains something of an ordeal. The final offensive, which broke the German Army in Italy only came in April 1945. The new commander, General Heinrich Vietinghof, was forced by Hitler to stand and fight south of the River Po holding a position around Bologna. The obvious stratagem would have been to retreat behind the river and fall back into the Alps. But the Führer was having none of it. The result was predictable. The demoralised German army was battered by massed artillery and air attack before being outflanked and surrounded. It was all over in three weeks. On 2 May Alexander received the surrender of all German forces in the area.

Mussolini, meanwhile, had decided that he would make his getaway to Switzerland. Accompanying him on his travels was his mistress, Clara Petacci, his brother Marcello and several other ministers and top fascists. The area was infested with partisans and getting past them was going to be tricky; in fact the inevitable happened as they were stopped at a roadblock and taken into partisan hands. They were not about to show leniency after all the misery that Mussolini had inflicted on his country. On 28 May 1945 the ex-dictator and his mistress were executed by sub-machine gun.

The next day their corpses were taken to a small suburban piazza in Milan where they were kicked and spat upon by a hysterical crowd before being hung upside down from girders. It was the same piazza where fifteen partisans had been executed ten months earlier.

For many it was just retribution.

95. HITLER MAKES HIS FAREWELL

Since the beginning of 1945 Hitler had retreated into his bunker in Berlin. From there he gave out increasingly frantic orders to phantom armies, which had already disintegrated in the face of Allied firepower and overwhelming numbers.

With Soviet forces pressing in on the German capital his entourage wanted the Führer to escape down to the south and make a last stand in the Bavarian mountains. However, Hitler was determined to go down 'heroically' in Berlin. On 21 April he once again flew into one of his uncontrollable rages. He claimed he was surrounded by cowardice, treachery and incompetence. Suddenly, to the astonishment of those around him he collapsed in a pool of tears and cried, 'The war is lost! Everything is falling apart.'

With the dictator increasingly cut off in his bunker, his closest colleagues outside the capital began considering ways of making the most of the deteriorating situation. First of all, Goering, who was officially Hitler's deputy, sent a telegram asking him if he still had 'freedom of action' and if not, he, Goering, would take control of the Reich. Hitler immediately saw red and had him stripped of all his offices.

The next up was Himmler, his 'trusty Heinrich', who, it was revealed, was secretly negotiating terms with Count Bernadotte of Sweden and was offering unconditional surrender of all German troops to the Western Allies. Hitler was stunned by this and ordered someone to arrest him forthwith. It really was all falling apart.

Before his final demise there were two things Hitler wanted to do: make a final testament and marry his mistress, Eva Braun – and in that order. After that he would commit suicide rather than fall into Allied hands and suffer a similar fate to his old playmate Mussolini.

Hitler dictated his testament to his youngest secretary, Traudl Junge. He claimed he had always loved his people and had never wanted war but it had been foisted on him by the Jews. The army had betrayed him and the Luftwaffe were not much better, and so he wanted Grand Admiral Dönitz to take over as president of the Reich after his death. He then set out his intention to make an honest woman of his mistress before their double suicide, much to Junge's astonishment.

There was one problem about tying the knot, however: there was nobody to officiate at the ceremony. Luckily, Goebbels, who loyally stayed with Hitler, managed to get hold of a notary who was fighting in Berlin. Afterwards the newlyweds celebrated with champagne and sandwiches. However, it was rather difficult to offer them a bright future!

On the next day, 30 April, a rather elderly-looking Hitler lined up his staff and shook hands with them before entering his private room with his wife. Some time later a shot rang out. The dictator had killed himself and beside him on the sofa lay Eva Braun, who had swallowed a cyanide capsule. Later their bodies were burned.

The next day Goebbels and his wife Magda sadly murdered their six children before also committing suicide.

96. Germany Surrenders Twice

After the death of Hitler it was only a matter of time before all Nazi forces surrendered. There were pockets of encircled German units right across Europe. However, not all of them were keen to throw in the towel. In Eastern Europe in particular some enemy armies were determined to fight on. This was because they preferred to surrender to the Western Allies rather than the Soviets, whose vengeance the Germans feared.

Montgomery was the first to receive a partial surrender in Germany itself. After crossing the Rhine at the end of March he had taken his British armies north-east in the direction of Denmark. They had made rapid progress and had reached Hamburg on the coast by the last week of April. Admiral Dönitz, now president of the Reich, sent a delegation to discuss terms of surrender, which would include German armies still fighting in the East. Monty could not risk offending the Soviets and so insisted that only troops in northern Germany, Holland and Denmark could surrender to him and that it should be unconditional. Eventually, on 4 May at Lüneberg Heath, the instrument of surrender was signed by a Dönitz's representative. Other ceremonies soon followed in southern Germany. Although this was momentous it was not the end.

Eisenhower, the Supreme Allied Commander in the West, demanded a full and complete surrender ceremony for all German forces be held in Reims, France, where Ike had his headquarters. The special event took place at 2.41 a.m. on 7 May. General Alfred Jodl duly signed on behalf of the German High Command with representatives of the Western Allies and the Soviet Union signing afterwards. Eisenhower decided not to attend the ceremony so as not to offer any respect to those Germans present. When

Churchill was awoken in London with the news by a certain Captain Richard Pim, the great man replied 'For five years you've brought me bad news, sometimes worse than others. Now you've redeemed yourself.'

Unfortunately, a few hours later the Soviet High Command contacted Eisenhower to say that Moscow would not recognise the ceremony and wanted a separate one. Stalin claimed they were still fighting in the East and the surrender at Reims did not sufficiently recognise the supreme effort of the Russian people. Stalin wanted the new ceremony on 8 May in Berlin. Eisenhower agreed.

In the end the Berlin ceremony took place at 1 a.m. on 9 May. Present was Field-Marshal Wilhelm Keitel, Chief of the German General Staff, Marshal Georgy Zhukov, representing the Soviet High Command, as well as other Allied representatives. It was a much more formal and impressive ceremony than Reims

Eisenhower had hoped to keep the first signing secret for thirty-six hours so that general celebrations could take place at the same time right across Europe. But the news leaked out early and so VE (Victory in Europe) Day was celebrated on 8 May in the West and 9 May in the Soviet Union.

97. THE HOLOCAUST WAS AN UNSPEAKABLE HORROR

We have seen that the Holocaust was not fully implemented until after the Wannsee conference in January 1942 (Fact 37). From that period until the end of the war the Nazi regime set about the extermination of the Jewish race in Europe. Never before in history have so many people been subjected to such a methodical and clinical destruction. It was mass murder on an industrial scale resulting in the estimated deaths of 5.7 million Jews. It is a genocide that should never be forgotten.

By 1942 Jews across Europe had already been subjected to ad hoc killings in Russia by *Einsatzgruppen* while many others were forced to live in ghettoes. The intensification of the 'Final Solution' required the victims to be transported wholesale to concentration camps specially set aside for the process. There were already camps across Europe, but these were often holding places for enemies of the state, for example those who may be murdered or suffer horrific privations but who did have a chance of survival. In the new camps the aim was liquidation. In such notorious places as Treblinka, Sobibór and Auschwitz (all in Poland) there was expected to be no escape.

Most Jewish people were cynically told they were going for resettlement in the East and were allowed to bring up to 25 kilograms of belongings. On the long journey in cattle trucks of up to eleven days they were provided with little food or water. On arrival at Birkenau, for example, there would be a *selektion* at which point only fit men and women would be sent off to work while the old, weak, and mothers with children would be immediately despatched to the 'showers'. Once inside, Zyklon B gas pellets would be dropped in and a wretched death would result within thirty minutes. Around 230,000 children died in this camp alone. The 'lucky' more able internees could expect to die through overwork, disease or arbitrary execution. Life expectancy was just six months.

Life in the camps was a daily test of survival. Over the entrance was written *'Arbeit macht frei'* (Work sets you free), but this was a cruel joke. Instead work in the factories of death was expected to grind people down until they could do no more and then they would be sent to the 'shower' blocks. In the camps the SS guards knew no bounds to their sadistic cruelty.

Liberation came in 1945 but for many it was too late. In Poland, ahead of the Soviet advance, many Jews had to suffer forced marches westwards in sub-zero temperatures. The usual executions were meted out for those who could not keep up and from Auschwitz 15,000 died in this way. Across the Nazi empire hundreds of those saved were too starved and malnourished to survive their day of freedom.

Many of the camp guards escaped punishment. However Adolf Eichmann, who was in charge of the deportations and concentration camps in Eastern Europe, was later captured in Argentina, put on trial in Israel in 1962 and afterwards hanged.

98. The Japanese Surrender as the World Goes Atomic

The people of Britain, America, France and the Soviet Union had marked VE Day with joyful celebrations. However, as Churchill had noted at the time, there was still another unfinished war in the Far East against the empire of Japan. Although the war was clearly lost, the military leadership there was determined to fight on until the last man standing. By May 1945 the Japanese mainland was being constantly pummelled by American B-52 bombers while the destruction of her merchant fleet and a naval blockade meant starvation for her people was perhaps only months away.

Estimates for an invasion of the Japanese mainland varied, but the Joint Chiefs of Staff put it at over a million US personnel killed and wounded. It could take months to secure final victory. However there was an alternative to this scenario. Since 1942 American scientists, with some assistance from the British and Canadians, had been working on the Manhattan Project, whose aim was to produce the first nuclear weapons. It was directed by Robert Oppenheimer and was based at Los Alamos in New Mexico. By July 1945 it was reckoned that the first two bombs could be ready by the beginning of the following month. The explosive power of these weapons was 2,000 times more than the largest bomb known to man.

In the end President Truman had few qualms about employing such terrible weapons. If their massive destructive power could convince the Japanese to surrender rather than fight on with the resultant loss of millions of lives on both sides then it had to be done. The first bomb to be dropped was codenamed Little Boy (named after Roosevelt). It was a uranium bomb that was loaded on to the B-29 Super fortress *Enola Gay* on 6 August 1945. At 8.15 a.m. the 8,000-lb bomb was released over the Japanese city of Hiroshima and forty-seven seconds later the people there were hit with a blast which, for a split second, generated 300,000 degrees Celsius. A mushroom-shaped cloud soon appeared over the city. The centre was literally vaporised and perhaps 140,000 people died in total with many suffering a prolonged death from radiation sickness.

The Japanese government was shocked by this but nevertheless decided to fight on in the hope that this was a one-off. So the Americans had another go to make their point. Three days later a plutonium bomb named Fat Boy (after Churchill) was released over Nagasaki killing over 70,000 people. At the same time the Soviet Union declared war. At this point even the most diehard nationalists had to admit the situation was hopeless. Emperor Hirohito agreed and broadcast to his people that unconditional surrender was the only option.

The surrender ceremony took place on Admiral Nimitz's flagship USS *Missouri*, which was anchored in Tokyo Bay. American and Allied top brass were there to see the high-ranking Japanese entourage, including its one-legged foreign minister, sign the surrender document. There was peace at last.

99. The Nurmberg Trial Brought a Measure of Justice

After the war the three great powers – Britain, America and the Soviet Union – decided that there should be special courts set up in order to bring to trial those in Germany and Japan who had been responsible for some of the worst crimes in history. In Tokyo a trial was held for those who had perpetrated massacres and terrible cruelties and some faced execution as a result. In occupied Germany, the Allies brought together twenty-three (two were missing) top Nazis, who were paraded before an international tribunal.

The star defendant was Hermann Goering. As the highest-ranking Nazi leader present he clearly took precedence and dominated his fellow defendants. He was suave and sophisticated and showed himself to be remarkably adroit and shrewd. He accepted full responsibility for his actions and made no apologies or excuses; indeed he said he was proud of his achievements. He denied that he was anti-Semitic and claimed to have no knowledge of the concentration camps.

Other defendants blamed the war and the horrors of the Holocaust on leaders who were conveniently dead: Hitler, Himmler and Heydrich. Many said they had no choice as they were just obeying orders. Others made statements that just failed to convince; for example, Ernst Kaltenbrunner, the highest-ranking member of the SS remaining, said 'I never killed anybody', and Wilhelm Keitel, the German Army's Chief of Staff for six years, claimed 'I was never really close to the Führer.' Some like Julius Streicher remained rabid Nazis to the end. Only Albert Speer, Hitler's chief architect and wartime armaments' minister, took full responsibility for the actions of the regime, although he denied having used slave labour.

Three of the accused were acquitted but most received death sentences to be carried out by hanging. Dönitz, the navy chief and Hitler's successor, was imprisoned for ten years while Speer was sent to prison for twenty. Rudolf Hess, the Nazi leader's rather deranged deputy (until 1940 when he flew solo to Scotland in a bid to get peace with Britain), got life imprisonment. Goering managed to outwit the hangman by getting an American GI he had befriended to sneak a cyanide capsule into his cell.

Of course, there were a myriad of other trials for lesser players but who nevertheless had committed horrific crimes. Interestingly, missing from the Nuremberg proceedings were the top-ranking German generals, including Manstein, who were complicit in the rounding-up and execution of Jews and communists on the Eastern front but who were never held to account. Their memoirs later tended to skate over certain inconvenient details. Indeed very few held to a chivalric code to which we imagine they belonged.

Goebbels once opined that the Nazi leadership would one day go down in history as the greatest statesmen or the greatest criminals. The latter is the case.

100. There Were Some Winners … and Some Losers

As peace extended over the world in 1945 it was clear to any onlooker who the victors and who the vanquished were. However, most of those who were seemingly victorious had suffered horrendously in a war of unparalleled destruction. Furthermore, some countries found themselves exchanging one foreign dictatorship for another one even though they were on the winning side.

Germany was clearly defeated. Unlike the Treaty of Versailles in 1919, when Germany escaped general occupation the three Allied powers and France took over the entire country. The German Reich was divided into four sectors with the Soviet Union taking the eastern part and the USA, Britain and France dividing up the western zone between them. Berlin was also divided up likewise. Japan, too, underwent general occupation, directed by the Americans under the jurisdiction of General Douglas MacArthur. President Truman deliberately excluded Russia as he was fearful of the extension of Soviet power.

America was clearly the greatest victor. She had not suffered occupation or bombing and had emerged as the world's first superpower. In addition, she was the possessor of the world's first nuclear weapons. Under the Marshall Plan she would use her wealth to restore a battered and prostrate Europe. Both West Germany and Japan would make remarkably rapid recoveries as a result of American largesse.

The Soviet Union, too, was a clear victor. She extended her frontiers westward and seized the Island of Sakhalin from Japan in the East. In addition to this, her troops occupied all of Eastern Europe and reached as far west as central Germany. But, of course the war had been devastating for the Soviet people, with many of their cities utterly destroyed and 27 million dead. The countries of Eastern Europe including the Baltic States, Poland, Czechoslovakia, Hungary, Rumania and Bulgaria now fell under the cloak of communist dictatorship and would stay so until 1989. Only Greece escaped this fate.

With hostility between the Western Allies and the Russia growing into a Cold War, Germany became permanently divided into East and West Germany until the collapse of the Soviet Union.

Britain was officially a winner, but was also a loser. She had gone to war to maintain her great power status but at the war's end she was clearly diminished and very soon had to suffer the dismemberment of her once mighty empire as the demands for independence mushroomed. France, too, was nominally a victor but would ultimately have to give up on her imperial pretensions. Ironically, the countries of Europe had gone to war to expand or maintain their empires, but it was their colonies that would finally emerge as winners. This is only just as they did make a massive contribution to Allied victory.

Perhaps the greatest legacy of the post-war settlement has been the lasting peace that has settled upon Europe and Japan from whence the terrible war originated.

Let us fervently hope it remains so!